WICKED
BUGS

Also by AMY STEWART

From the Ground Up:
The Story of a First Garden

The Earth Moved:
On the Remarkable Achievements of Earthworms

Flower Confidential:
The Good, the Bad, and the Beautiful in the Business of Flowers

Wicked Plants:
The Weed That Killed Lincoln's Mother &
Other Botanical Atrocities

Wicked Bugs:
The Louse That Conquered Napoleon's Army &
Other Diabolical Insects

WICKED BUGS

THE MEANEST, DEADLIEST, GROSSEST BUGS ON EARTH

AMY STEWART

Illustrated by Briony Morrow-Cribbs

ALGONQUIN YOUNG READERS   2017

Published by
Algonquin Young Readers
an imprint of Algonquin Books of Chapel Hill
Post Office Box 2225
Chapel Hill, North Carolina 27515-2225

a division of
Workman Publishing
225 Varick Street
New York, New York 10014

Design by Becky Terhune.

Library Of Congress Cataloging-in-Publication Data

Names: Stewart, Amy, author.
Title: Wicked bugs : the meanest, deadliest, grossest bugs on earth / Amy Stewart.
Description: First edition. | Chapel Hill, North Carolina :
Algonquin Young Readers, 2017. | Includes bibliographical references and index. |
Audience: Ages 8 to 12. | Audience: Grades 4 to 6.
Identifiers: LCCN 2017013260| ISBN 9781616206994 (pbk.) |
ISBN 9781616207557 (hardcover)
Subjects: LCSH: Insect pests—Juvenile literature. | Arachnida—Juvenile literature.
Classification: LCC SB931 .S83 2017 | DDC 632/.7—dc22
LC record available at https://lccn.loc.gov/2017013260

10 9 8 7 6 5 4 3 2 1
First Edition

To PSB

TABLE OF CONTENTS

WARNING: WE ARE SERIOUSLY OUTNUMBERED ix

**A BRIEF EXPLANATION OF
SCIENTIFIC CLASSIFICATION** xi

DEADLY CREATURES 1
Brazilian Wandering Spider 3
Tsetse Fly 7
Assassin Bug 11
Mosquito 17
Oriental Rat Flea 21
Curse of the Scorpion 24

EVERYDAY DANGERS 27
Cockroach 29
Deer Tick 33
Bed Bug 37
Body Lice 41
Head Lice 45
The Enemy Within 47

UNWELCOME INVADERS 53
Nightcrawler 55
Brown Marmorated Stink Bug 59
African Bat Bug 63
Millipede 67
Zombies 70

DESTRUCTIVE PESTS 73
Death-Watch Beetle 75
Rocky Mountain Locust 79
Mountain Pine Beetle 83
Formosan Subterranean Termite 87
Corpse Eaters 90

SERIOUS PAINS 95
Asian Giant Hornet 97
Paederus Beetle 101
Brown Recluse 105
Giant Centipede 109
Scabies Mite 113
Bombardier Beetle 117
Tarantula 121
Stinging Caterpillars 123
The Ants Go Marching 127

TERRIBLE THREATS 133
Black Widow 135
Chigoe Flea 139
Chigger Mite 143
Sand Fly 147
Black Fly 151
Filth Fly 155
I've Got You Under My Skin 158

FEAR OF BUGS 164

GLOSSARY 165

RESOURCES 167

BIBLIOGRAPHY 170

INDEX 172

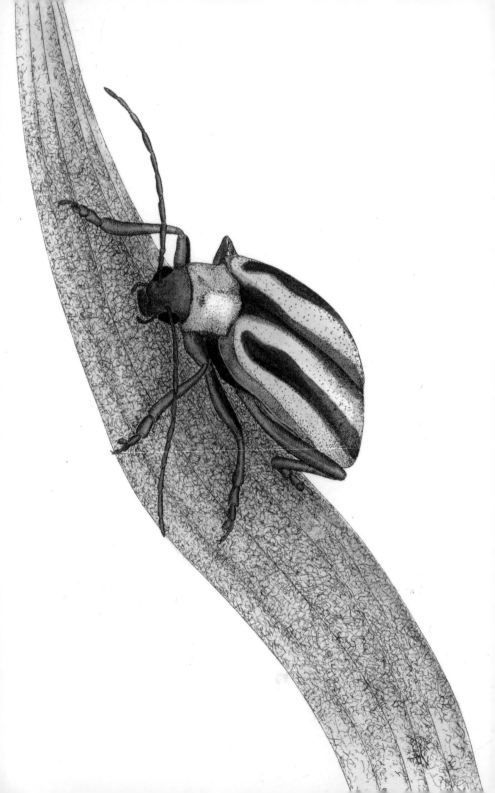

WARNING: WE ARE SERIOUSLY OUTNUMBERED

In 1909, the *Chicago Daily Tribune* ran an article titled "If Bugs Were the Size of Men." The reporter asked what would happen "if some mighty magician's wand should be waved over the world tomorrow and mankind be reduced to the size of insects, while these tiny creatures should reach the size of men."

The article imagined what it would be like if humans traded places with bugs: the giant Hercules beetle was not just tough, but immoral, with a taste for drinking and fighting; bark beetles would mow down massive fortresses; armies would be helpless against the weapons of the bombardier beetle; and spiders would "destroy elephants . . . a man's only possible salvation would be that he was too insignificant to attack." Even lions would cower in fear against these new winged and multilegged enemies.

The reporter's intent was, undoubtedly, to make the point that insects are powerful in their own way, and that it is only their size that keeps them from conquering the world.

In fact, insects have changed the course of history. They have halted soldiers in their tracks. They have driven farmers off their land. They have devoured cities and forests, and inflicted pain, suffering, and death upon hundreds of millions.

This is not to say that they don't do good as well. They pollinate the plants that feed us, and they are themselves food for creatures up and down the food chain. They do the vital work of decomposition, returning everything from fallen leaves to fallen heroes back to the earth. Many insects, from the blow fly to the blister beetle, have proven useful in medicine. And insects prey on one another, keeping pests in check. We could not live without them. In fact, indiscriminate pesticide use and destruction of their habitats is far more harmful than simply learning to live alongside them and appreciate their better qualities.

Entomologists, the scientists who study insects, will quickly protest that the term "bug" is misleading, and they are right. Most of us use the word to describe any number of tiny slithering and crawling creatures. Strictly speaking, an insect is a creature with six legs, a three-segmented body, and usually two sets of wings. A true bug is a subset of insect in the order Hemiptera that has piercing and sucking mouthparts. An aphid, therefore, is a type of insect that we can properly call a bug; an ant is not. Spiders, worms, centipedes, slugs, and scorpions are not insects at all but arachnids and other classes of creatures that are only distantly related to insects. But for the sake of simplicity, this book uses the amateur's definition of the term "bug" to refer to them all.

To date, over one million species of insects have been described worldwide. It is estimated that there are ten quintillion insects alive on the planet right now, which means that for each one of us, there are two hundred million of them. If you arranged all living creatures on earth into a pyramid, almost all of it would be made up of insects, spiders, and the like. Animals and people would form only the smallest section in one corner of the pyramid. We are seriously outnumbered.

A BRIEF EXPLANATION OF SCIENTIFIC CLASSIFICATION

Scientists put all living creatures into seven levels of classification. For example, here is the scientific classification for humans:

Kingdom: Animalia

Phylum: Chordata

Class: Mammalia

Order: Primates

Family: Hominidae

Genus: Homo

Species: sapiens

The scientific name of a living creature is its genus followed by its species, such as *Homo sapiens* for humans.

When a writer is referring generally to any species within the same genus, she might give just the genus name followed by the abbreviation *sp.*, which stands for *species* and indicates that the writer is not referring to any particular species. The abbreviation *spp.* means that the writer is referring to several species at once. You'll see both abbreviations in this book. The mosquito on page 17 is referred to as *Anopheles sp.* This means that the information found within the chapter is not limited to any particular species of mosquito.

WICKED BUGS

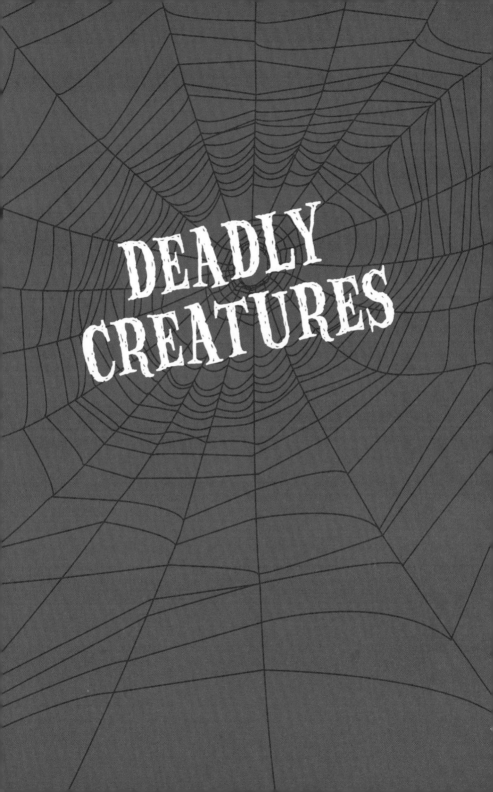

DEADLY CREATURES

BRAZILIAN WANDERING SPIDER
Phoneutria sp.

I t was a normal day at the Rio de Janeiro airport. Luggage rolled smoothly through the security checkpoint, the X-ray machines revealing the usual assortment of bikinis and sandals and suntan lotion. But the contents of one suitcase brought the entire checkpoint to a halt. Judging from the image on the X-ray machine, the suitcase appeared to hold hundreds of tiny, twisted legs.

SIZE: 6 in (15 cm) including legs

FAMILY: Ctenidae

HABITAT: Jungles, rain forests, and dark, secluded areas like woodpiles and sheds

DISTRIBUTION: Central and South America

MEET THE RELATIVES: Members of the Ctenidae family are generally ground-dwelling spiders that hunt rather than spin webs.

Someone was trying to sneak deadly spiders out of Brazil! The suitcase was carefully packed with tiny white boxes, each one holding a single live spider. The smuggler was a young Welshman who claimed he was bringing them back to Wales to sell in his spider shop. A complete search of his luggage turned up a thousand spiders in all. He even packed them in his carry-on bag. Brazilian security officials remarked that had the spiders escaped and started dropping down from the overhead bins during the flight, the chaos would have been unimaginable.

For identification the spiders were sent to a laboratory, where it became clear that these were no ordinary arachnids. One of the

Had the spiders escaped and started dropping down from the overhead bins during the flight, the chaos would have been unimaginable.

species the Welshman had collected was the Brazilian wandering spider, believed to be among the most dangerous in the world.

This large, grayish-brown spider is unusual since it doesn't spin a web and wait for prey to blunder into it. Instead, it prowls the floor of the jungle and even walks through the city, hunting for dinner late into the night. And while most spiders will scurry away at the sight of an aggressor, the Brazilian wandering spider stands its ground, rising up on its hind legs to get ready for a fight. Anyone who swats at one of these spiders had better aim to kill, because if it survives a swat with a broom, it might try to climb straight up the handle and bite.

The spider's bite causes a flood of immediate and severe pain, which can be followed by difficulty breathing, paralysis, and even asphyxiation. People who suspect that they've been bitten by a Brazilian wandering spider must seek immediate medical attention, but with proper care and a little luck they will survive.

There are eight species of wandering spiders. They are all found throughout parts of Central and South America and are recognizable for their eight eyes, four of which form a box shape directly in the front of their face. The eight species are not all equally venomous, and when bitten, most people suffer only mild pain and recover fully. However, the most venomous species are capable of killing, with young children and the elderly at the greatest risk.

The spider has earned the nickname "banana spider" because it sometimes climbs around in banana trees hunting for prey and ends up as a stowaway in shipments of fruit. There are many harmless look-alike species that turn up in bananas and other cargo as well, and only a few scientists around the world are capable of making an accurate identification. It is difficult, therefore, to rely on media accounts of Brazilian wandering spider bites inflicted by spiders in imported produce. Nonetheless, a British chef unpacking a box of bananas in the kitchen was reportedly bitten by one in 2005. Despite the pain and shock, he managed to grab his cell phone and snap a picture of the spider. The spider itself was later found in the kitchen, allowing experts to identify it and give the man the right course of treatment. He survived, but only after spending a week in the hospital.

TSETSE FLY
Glossina sp.

In 1742, a surgeon named John Atkins described a condition he called "the Sleepy Distemper." It afflicted people taken from West Africa and enslaved, and it seemed to come on with no warning other than a loss of appetite, followed by a state of sleep so deep that not even a beating would awake them. "Their Sleeps are sound," he wrote, "and Sense of Feeling very little; for pulling, drubbing, or whipping, will scarce stir up Sense and Power enough to move; and the Moment you cease beating the Smart is forgot, and down they fall again into a State of Insensibility."

SIZE: $1/4$–$1/2$ in (6–13 mm)

FAMILY: Glossinidae

HABITAT: Rain forests, savanna woodlands, and thickets

DISTRIBUTION: Africa, particularly in the south

MEET THE RELATIVES: There are about twenty-five species of tsetse flies, and they make up the entire Glossinidae family.

It did not occur to Atkins to investigate the activities of a large, annoying fly that made a *tse-tse* sound as it buzzed around. It would be over a hundred years before the true cause of sleeping sickness was known.

The tsetse fly is found primarily in Africa south of the Sahara desert. Both male and female flies require blood meals to survive. There are about thirty species of the fly, which attack humans on different parts of their bodies. *Glossina morsitans*, for instance, will bite anywhere, while *Glossina palpalis* prefers to feed above the waist, and *Glossina tachinoides* generally attacks below the knee. Most tsetse flies are attracted to bright colors, so wearing neutral clothing is one way to ward them off.

The flies feed on the blood of wild game, livestock, and humans, sometimes transmitting the protozoa that cause sleeping sickness from one infected creature to the next. The first symptom is an extreme swelling of the lymph nodes, masses of tissue in the body. The infection finds its way into the central nervous system and brain, causing irritability, fatigue, aches, personality changes, confusion, and slurred speech. Left untreated, a person may be dead within six months, usually from heart failure.

He left an epidemic of sleeping sickness in his wake that wiped out as much as two-thirds of the region's population.

Although the fly has been around for at least thirty-four million years, the disease it transmits was mentioned only occasionally in early medical writings. It was not until European explorers began moving large expeditions of animals and workers through the African continent that sleeping sickness, called trypanosomiasis, became widespread and better understood. Journalist and British explorer Henry Morton Stanley traveled through Uganda in the late nineteenth century with a large party of cattle and men. They were followed by the tsetse fly, which accompanied the expedition because of the easy food source. He left an epidemic of sleeping sickness in his wake that wiped out as much as two-thirds of the region's population.

There are two forms of the disease, one found in East Africa and another found in West Africa. It is estimated that fifty to seventy thousand people may be infected with the disease today, but that number was ten times as high just a decade ago.

One strategy for controlling the disease focuses on the tsetse fly itself. Scientists at the International Atomic Energy Agency have found some success with a "sterile insect technique" that involves raising male flies in a laboratory, exposing them to radiation to render them sterile, then releasing them to mate with females, which would then finish their life cycle without actually reproducing.

ASSASSIN BUG
Triatoma infestans

In 1835, Charles Darwin, the English scientist whose theory of evolution helped demonstrate that humans and other creatures evolved from a common ancestor, recorded a strange encounter with a bug in Argentina. He was near the end of his journey on board the HMS *Beagle*, a British naval ship charged with surveying South America. Darwin had been hired to fulfill the role of scholarly companion to the captain and ship's naturalist. The journey had already been fraught with peril: the captain was unstable and ill-tempered; the locals attacked the crew and robbed them; and most everyone suffered illness or hunger at some point. Then, on March 25, Darwin himself became dinner for one of the region's bloodsucking insects. In his diary he wrote: "At night I experienced an attack (for it deserves no less a name) of the Benchuca, a species of Reduvius, the great

SIZE: ½–1 in (1.3–2.5 cm)

FAMILY: Reduviidae

HABITAT: Generally found near prey, which could mean homes, barns, nests, caves, or any shelters where birds, rodents, and other mammals live

DISTRIBUTION: North and South America; some species in India and Southeast Asia

MEET THE RELATIVES: Wheel bugs, which prey upon caterpillars and other garden pests, are a type of assassin bug. Other relatives include the so-called thread-legged bugs, a group of long, skinny insects whose victims include spiders and other insects.

black bug of the Pampas. It is most disgusting to feel soft wingless insects, about an inch long, crawling over one's body."

He also recounted an experiment in which several of his shipmates offered themselves up to the bloodthirsty beasts: "When placed on a table, and though surrounded by people, if a finger was presented, the bold insect would immediately protrude its sucker, make a charge, and if allowed, draw blood . . . This one feast, for which the benchuca was indebted to one of the officers, kept it fat during four whole months."

What Darwin didn't know—what no one knew at the time—was that the bite of some assassin bugs can transmit a fatal illness called Chagas disease. There are about 138 species of these large, oval-shaped, bloodsucking insects worldwide, half of which are known to transmit the disease. Most are found in North and South America, although there are some species in India and Southeast Asia. They live quite comfortably alongside their hosts, hiding out in burrows and nests and feeding on the small rodents or bats that live in them. They're not shy about moving into houses or barns, either. In some parts of Latin America, where palm fronds are used as roofing material, the bugs are accidentally introduced into local households through eggs attached to the fronds.

Assassin bugs go through five nympha stages on their way to adulthood, drinking up to nine times their weight in blood during a single feeding. An adult female may live six months, and during that time, she'll lay one hundred to six hundred eggs, the precise number depending on how much blood she consumes.

In most cases, the bite of the assassin bug causes no pain. It may feed for just a few minutes or up to half an hour, its body growing engorged as it drinks. A home with a severe infestation may contain several hundred bugs. In this case, it would not be uncommon for as many as twenty bugs to feed on an individual person, taking one to three milliliters of blood per night, a little more than half a teaspoon. Health-care workers visiting the homes of their patients recognize the worst infestations by the black-and-white streaks of waste products running down the walls.

The assassin bug's preference for feeding around the mouth of its victim has earned it the nickname "kissing bug." Unfortunately, it can be the kiss of death.

In 1908, a Brazilian doctor named Carlos Chagas was studying malaria when he noticed this bloodsucking insect and decided to find out whether it was carrying any disease-causing microbes. What he found was a protozoan parasite

The assassin bug's preference for feeding around the mouth of its victim has earned it the nickname "kissing bug." Unfortunately, it can be the kiss of death.

that the bug takes in during a meal. The parasite develops and multiplies inside the gut of the bug, and is then excreted in its feces. People get infected not from the bite itself but from the feces deposited on the skin of the victim while the bug feeds. Scratching or rubbing the bug bite pushes the waste into the wound, introducing it into the bloodstream. (North American assassin bugs wait to do their business about a half hour after they have eaten, by which time they have moved away from the victim. This helps explain why the disease is less common in the United States.)

What is most remarkable about Chagas's discovery is that he found the disease inside the vector insect, the organism that carries the disease from one host to another, first. Then he went on to diagnose humans who were infected with it. This process was unusual because scientists usually trace a disease back from infected human beings to the animals they came in contact with. Chagas realized that he'd stumbled across a fatal disease that seemed to be linked to colonization. As settlers cleared land in the jungle and built mud and palm-thatched huts, the assassin bugs that were already living in the jungle and carrying the disease from one rodent to another found themselves suddenly living among humans—a fantastic source of warm, rich blood. Although the locals had already named the bug—some called it *vinchuca*, which means "that which lets itself fall" from the roof; others called it *Chitimacha*, which means "that which fears the cold"—the disease caused by the bug was just starting to become widespread around the time Dr. Chagas discovered it.

People who are bitten by infected bugs around the eyes develop a terrible swelling. Bites elsewhere on the body result in small sores that give way to fever and swollen lymph nodes. Chagas disease can kill in its early stages. Most people go on to experience a symptom-less phase, followed by extensive damage to the heart, intestines, and other major organs, which may ultimately be fatal. About three hundred thousand people in the United States live with Chagas disease, and eight to eleven million people throughout Latin America suffer from it. Although early treatment can kill the parasites, there is no treatment for the later stages of the disease.

Some historians speculate that Charles Darwin himself was infected with Chagas disease and ultimately died from it. This would explain some of the strange and complicated health problems that plagued him throughout his life. However, the fact that he seems to have suffered from some of the same symptoms before he encountered the assassin bug in Argentina argues against that theory. Requests to exhume his remains from Westminster Abbey and test them for Chagas disease have been denied, leaving the exact cause of his health problems a mystery.

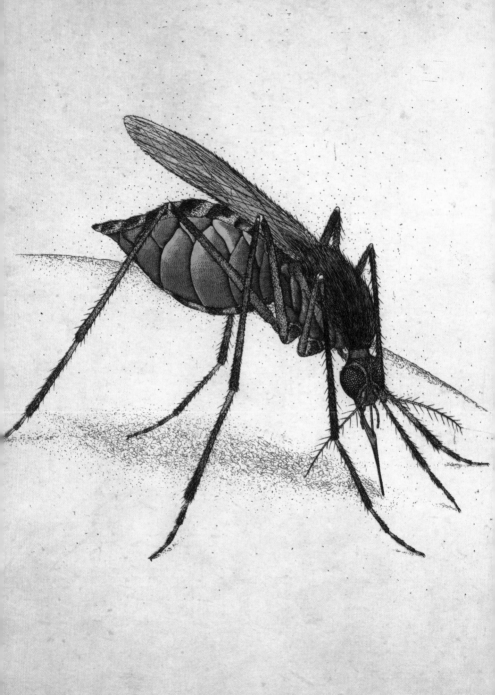

MOSQUITO
Anopheles sp.

SIZE: Wing length $1/8$ in (3 mm)

FAMILY: Culicidae

HABITAT: Varies widely, but usually found around bodies of water, from lakes to marshes to isolated pools

DISTRIBUTION: Tropical, subtropical, and some temperate climates worldwide

MEET THE RELATIVES: All mosquitoes are found in the family Culicidae. There are roughly 3000 species, 150 of which live in North America.

On July 10, 1783, just as the Revolutionary War was coming to an end, George Washington, American general and commander in chief of the colonial armies, wrote to his nephew that "Mrs. Washington has had three of the Ague & fever & is much with it."

The "Ague & fever" that the future first president of the United States was referring to was malaria, a disease that had plagued him since he was a teenager and also infected his wife. He suffered several bouts of it over the years, along with smallpox, typhoid fever, pneumonia, and influenza. The treatment for malaria was quinine, extracted from the bark of the South American cinchona tree. Although quinine was already in use in Europe, it didn't reach the Washingtons until later in life. Unfortunately, the president took so much of the drug that it caused severe hearing loss during the second year of his first term.

Malaria has been called our "forever enemy." Tests on mosquitoes preserved in amber from thirty million years ago show that it predates humans. The earliest medical texts refer to a "malarial fever," and some even suggested that an insect bite could be the cause. The word *malaria*, however, comes from the Italian word for "bad air" and suggests the commonly held belief that malaria was simply present in the air.

As we now know, mosquitoes are to blame. They transmit not just malaria but dengue fever, yellow fever, Rift Valley fever, and about a hundred other human diseases. Roughly one in five of all insect-transmitted diseases come from mosquitoes, making them the world's deadliest insect. Malaria is believed to have killed more people than all wars combined.

Malaria is caused by four species of microscopic parasites that cause different strains of malaria. It's spread only by female mosquitoes, since males don't feed on blood. First, the mosquitoes become infected by feeding on an infected host and taking in male and

Malaria is believed to have killed more people than all wars combined.

female parasites along with the blood. Next, the parasites reproduce in the mosquito's body, and within several days, they make their way to the salivary glands, which create saliva. Because mosquitoes live only a few weeks, they may not survive long enough for this to happen. But if it does happen, and they then feed on someone else, the disease cycle continues. The mosquitoes inject saliva into their victim, thereby stopping the blood from clotting by acting as an anticoagulant. If enough parasites are present in the mosquito's saliva, the victim may become infected—but it is possible to be bitten by an infected mosquito and not get malaria.

Mosquitoes are attracted to their hosts by carbon dioxide, lactic acid, and octenol, which are found in human sweat and breath. They also sense heat and humidity around a body. They like dark colors, and they seem to be drawn to people who have been exercising. Scientists believe that there are other, not-yet-identified compounds that draw the bloodsuckers, including the food a person eats or an enticing mixture of perfumes, soaps, and other fragrances.

When a mosquito feeds, she goes through a four-stage process. First, she explores the skin with a sharp mouthpart called her proboscis. She's looking for a spot that has plenty of blood and is easy to get to. She then penetrates the upper layers of skin, hunting for a blood vessel. The saliva she discharges prevents blood from clotting. Once she finds a vessel, she starts drawing blood, feeding for up to four minutes. Then she pushes away and flies off a short distance to digest her meal.

Simply getting bitten by a mosquito can be annoying and irritating, but a bite can also be dangerous. Multiple bites and scratches can lead to secondary infections from bacteria. In Yangon, Myanmar, residents can get as many as eighty thousand bites per year. In northern Canada, when mosquito populations are high, people can get bit as many as 280 to 300 times per minute. At this rate, it would take a swarm of mosquitoes only ninety minutes to drain half the blood from a human body.

Today, 41 percent of the world's population lives in an area where malaria can be caught. There are nearly five hundred million cases worldwide annually, and every year over a million people die, most of them young children in sub-Saharan Africa, the area of the continent that is south of the Sahara desert. Experts estimate that controlling malaria worldwide would cost $3 billion. Bed nets play a critical role in protecting people at night when mosquitoes are active. Drugs including quinine are also an important strategy in treating the disease. Currently, there is no vaccine.

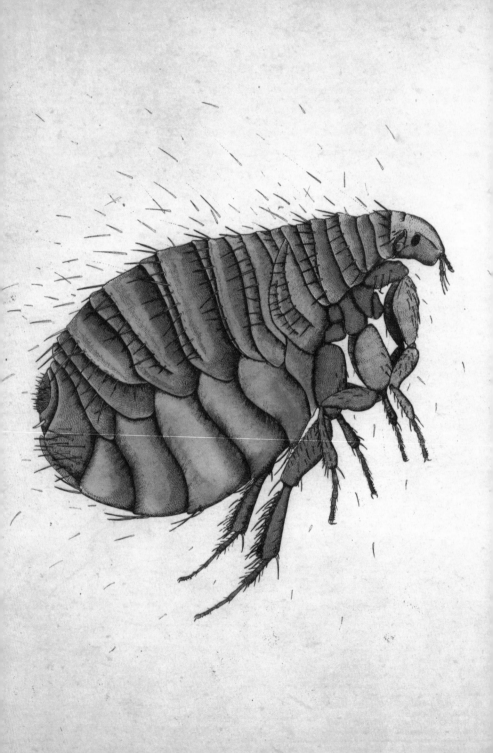

ORIENTAL RAT FLEA
Xenopsylla cheopis

O
n an autumn day in 1907, two brothers in San Francisco found a dead rat in the cellar. Inspired by their father, an undertaker, they decided to find a coffin for the rat to give it a proper funeral. When they ran home for dinner that night, the boys brought along a souvenir of their adventures—bloodthirsty fleas, starved for a meal after their rat host had died. Along with the fleas came a deadly disease—the plague.

SIZE: Up to $1/6$ in (4 mm)

FAMILY: Pulicidae

HABITAT: Near rats, their primary food source

DISTRIBUTION: Worldwide, particularly tropical and subtropical climates, but some temperate zones as well

MEET THE RELATIVES: The cat flea, *Ctenocephalides felis*, is a relative, as is the dog flea *C. canis*—but in the United States, it is primarily the cat flea that preys on both cats and dogs. They are known to transmit tapeworms.

The rat flea would prefer to leave humans, cats, dogs, and chickens alone, but when rat populations experience a massive die-off—as they do during epidemics of the plague—the fleas turn to other warm-blooded creatures for their food. This is exactly what happened to those two unfortunate boys. Within a month, the plague had killed their parents but spared the boys, leaving them orphans.

This particular rat had died during an outbreak of the Black Death that began just after the turn of the twentieth century. A steamer called the *Australia* left Honolulu, Hawaii, and passed through San Francisco's Golden Gate with its load of passengers, mail, and plague-ridden rats. The rats made their way through the city, which, at that time, was not a clean place. Garbage piled up, and makeshift sewers allowed germs and rodents to multiply. The rats felt right at home. Soon, a few people exhibited the dreaded symptoms of the plague—severe fever and chills, headaches and body pain, and telltale red lumps the size of boiled eggs in their armpits and groins. Before long, bleeding would give way to enormous black bruises, and death would not be far behind.

The flea's role in this dreaded disease had been discovered in the late 1800s, but the exact mechanism was still a mystery. It was not until 1914 that scientists realized that the gut of the flea held clues as to how it managed to spread the plague so swiftly and efficiently. They discovered a phenomenon called blocking, in which the plague bacteria build up in the gut of a flea to such an extent that the flea can barely swallow. Instead, it is only able to draw the host's blood into its esophagus, the part of the body that runs from its throat to its stomach. There the blood mingles with live plague bacteria. Unable to swallow because it is so full of plague itself, the flea regurgitates the blood and the bacteria back into the host's bloodstream. Flea vomit is the true culprit in a plague epidemic.

But that's not all. The fleas are so hungry because of their inability to digest a blood meal that they feed voraciously, moving from host to host in a desperate attempt to fill their bellies. Ultimately, the fleas die of starvation and exhaustion—if the plague itself doesn't kill them first.

The Oriental rat flea is just one of over eighty species of fleas that transmit the plague. The disease would have killed many more San Francisco residents during the so-called Barbary Plague except for one lucky fact: Oriental rat fleas were in the minority during this outbreak. The species most often found during the San Francisco plague were less likely to engage "blocking" and less likely to regurgitate plague bacteria.

The plague appears to have evolved from a more benign gastrointestinal bug about twenty thousand years ago. It has run its destructive course through human civilization several times, reputed to have killed more people than all wars combined in the course of human history. An African and European pandemic in the sixth century known as Justinian's plague killed about forty million people, which represented about a fifth of the world's population at that time. When it reappeared in Europe in the Middle Ages, the plague was called the Black Death. For two centuries, it ravaged Europe, killing another one-third to one-half of the continent's population.

Flea vomit is the true culprit in a plague epidemic.

Doctors at the time believed that the plague circulated in the air. They ordered patients to keep their windows closed and refrain from bathing, which they believed would expose the skin to the sickening air. Keeping the windows closed wouldn't stop the plague, but it might have stopped the stench of the dead and the dying. In large cities like London, there was no choice but to pile bodies in thinly covered mass graves. The rat population thrived in such a horrific mess. And because cats were believed to be witch companions in the Middle Ages, they were killed, nearly eliminating one of the rat's natural predators just when Europeans could have used the cats' hunting skills the most.

The plague then moved from China to India to the United States in the early twentieth century. Today, cases of the plague still occur from time to time in the American Southwest, but modern antibiotics can usually treat a case that is caught early.

CURSE OF THE SCORPION

A scorpion bite may be painful, but it's almost never fatal—for adults. Children are another matter. A California couple vacationing in Puerto Vallarta in 1994 learned this the hard way when their thirteen-month-old child stepped on a scorpion that had been hiding in his shoe. The boy started crying and frothing at the mouth, and soon developed a high fever. At a local emergency room, he stopped breathing a few times. Finally, his parents called a San Diego hospital and had him flown there, where he was placed on life support. He did survive, but even hospital staffers weren't sure he would make it.

In a small child, the neurotoxic venom of a scorpion can cause seizures, loss of muscle control, and unbearable pain all over the body as it goes to work on the nerves.

Fortunately, at the Phoenix Children's Hospital, parents are offered the choice of sedation for their child, or an antivenin called Anascorp. The drug is administered intravenously and starts working within a couple of hours, usually allowing the victim to go home with pain medications the same day. This breakthrough is being cheered in Arizona, where eight thousand people are stung every year, two hundred of them small children who suffer serious side effects.

Scorpions glow under ultraviolet light, so Arizonans who wish to check under their beds for scorpions can use a black-light flashlight.

Scorpions are found in desert, tropical, and subtropical areas throughout the world, and over twelve hundred species of these arachnids have been identified. It is often difficult to prove that a particular species was responsible for a sting, unless the scorpion was captured and identified. But here are just a few to avoid:

ARIZONA BARK SCORPION *Centruroides sculpturatus:* This is the scorpion most feared by Arizonans. It lives in the southwestern United States and Mexico, nestling under rocks and piles of wood. It also makes its way into homes. At only two and three-quarters to three inches (seven to eight centimeters) in length, the scorpion is easy to miss, especially since it is active at night. Fortunately, scorpions glow under ultraviolet light, so Arizonans who wish to check under their beds for scorpions can use a black-light flashlight, which is often marketed as a scorpion-hunting tool. The sting is considered to be the most painful of any scorpion in the United States, lasting for up to seventy-two hours.

DEATHSTALKER *Leiurus quinquestriatus:* This is another Middle Eastern scorpion that soldiers are warned to avoid. This light yellow and beige scorpion is easy to overlook in sandy soil, but its venom is highly toxic. An Air Force medic who was stung twice had to be flown to a hospital, where she was put on life support and given an experimental antivenin to save her life.

FATTAIL SCORPION *Androctonus crassicauda:* This highly dangerous dark brown scorpion is found in Iraq and other Middle Eastern countries. It gets its name from its menacing, oversize tail. The military classifies it as one of the deadliest scorpions in the world and warns that it can cause death, by making the heart stop beating or by stopping a person from breathing.

TRINIDAD SCORPION *Tityus trinitatis:* Found around Trinidad and in Venezuela, these diminutive creatures reach only about two inches (five centimeters) in length but deliver a painful sting that can cause pancreatitis, an illness that damages the organ that helps digest food. The deaths of a few children have been attributed to the venom of this scorpion, usually due to damage to the myocardium, or heart muscle tissue.

WHIP SCORPION *Mastigoproctus giganteus:* This arachnid is also called a vinegarroon and is not technically a true scorpion. It uses an extraordinary piece of natural artillery to defend itself. Rather than sting its enemy, it sprays a liquid made of 84 percent acetic acid. Household vinegar is only 5 percent acetic acid, making this spray something like the strongest vinegar imaginable. What is most extraordinary about this defense is the fact that the scorpion can whip its tail around and spray in any direction, sending predators running for cover.

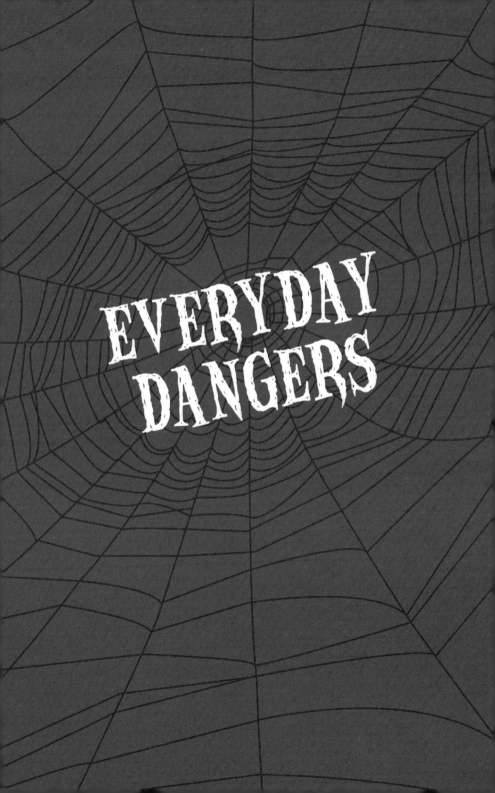

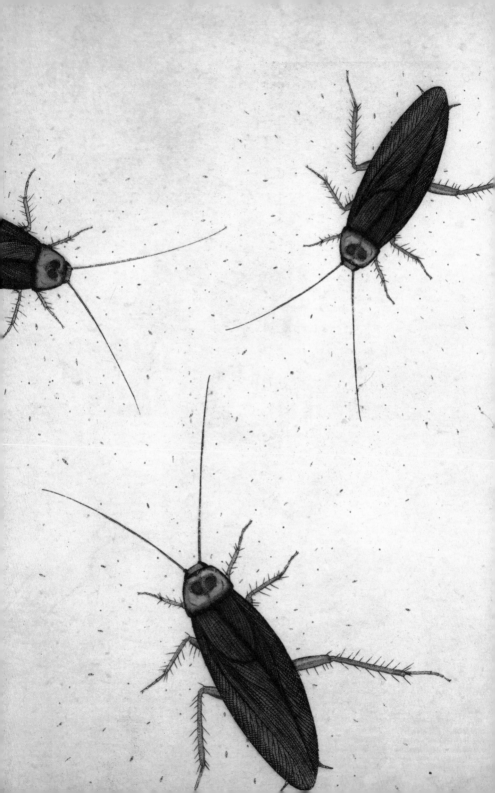

COCKROACH
Blattella germanica

As one of the oldest insects on the planet, dating back 350 million years, cockroaches have long been associated with humans. But in fact, of 4000 known species, 95 percent of them live entirely apart from humans—in forests, under logs, in caves, under rocks in the desert, and in damp, dark habitats near lakes and rivers. The 5 percent that do live around people seem to be universally loathed, for a number of reasons.

SIZE: Up to $5/8$ in (1.6 cm)

FAMILY: Blattellidae

HABITAT: Lives primarily around humans in homes and buildings

DISTRIBUTION: Worldwide

MEET THE RELATIVES: There are roughly 4000 species around the world. *Periplaneta americana*, the American cockroach, or palmetto bug, is a very large roach found throughout the southern United States and along parts of the East Coast.

Cockroaches have no trouble finding their way into any house. They do have wings, and some species are capable of short flights. They are known to land on a door and wait until it opens to get inside or to crawl in through any crack or opening. Whether they stay depends entirely upon housekeeping. They love a messy kitchen and bathroom, and once they're in an apartment complex, the shared heating ductwork, sewer lines, and electrical wiring in multiple dwellings mean that they can easily travel from one apartment to the next without ever going outside. One study showed that roaches in Arizona moved several hundred yards through sewer systems to enter a home. Once inside, cockroaches give off a telltale repulsive, musty odor.

They are omnivorous feeders, eating both vegetables and meat products. With what scientists call "unspecialized chewing mouthparts," they live alongside humans and feed off a wide variety of human waste. Spilled food, trash, and sewage all attract cockroaches, but they will even chew on bookbindings and the paste on stamps. Medical entomologists have reported that although cockroaches don't bite humans, they feed on "fingernails, eyelashes, skin, calluses on hands and feet, and food residues about the faces of sleeping humans."

As one of the oldest insects on the planet, dating back 350 million years, cockroaches have long been associated with humans.

All this shuttling between people, food, and garbage means that roaches carry any number of pathogens around with them, including *E. coli,* salmonella, leprosy, typhoid, dysentery, plague, hookworm, hepatitis, staphylococcus, and streptococcus. When cockroaches feed, they often throw up a little food from their crop, where they store the food after swallowing, leaving behind bits of their last meal as they eat the next one. They also defecate as they move and feed, leaving behind tiny brown droppings as small as flakes of pepper, all of which makes it easier for them to spread disease.

If that isn't bad enough, half of all people with asthma are allergic to cockroaches. Ten percent of nonallergic people also have some kind of sensitivity to cockroaches, with the most severe reactions causing anaphylactic shock. Roach allergens can survive the most thorough cleaning measures, including boiling water, changes to acidity, and ultraviolet light. Curiously, a cockroach allergy can bring on cross-reactions to crab, lobster, shrimp, and crawfish, as well as dust mites and other bugs.

But perhaps the most dreaded human-to-cockroach encounter is the legendary ear infestation. Although it sounds too horrible to be true, cases of cockroaches crawling into people's ears and getting stuck there have been well documented in medical literature. Emergency room doctors can pour oil in the ear to drown a cockroach, but they often have a hard time extracting it afterward. Some doctors swear by a squirt of lidocaine, which irritates the roach so much that it can send it running out of the ear and across the room.

Attempts to rid homes of cockroaches often lead to even more health problems. Epidemiologists have noted that an increase in home pesticide use, and the overall exposure to the chemicals that results from using them in the home, can pose a more serious hazard than the bugs themselves do. Safer roach baits are available, but cleanliness and a well-sealed home are the best defenses. A recent study showed that the "juice" of dead roaches is an effective roach repellent, but this is not likely to catch on as a home remedy.

DEER TICK
Ixodes scapularis

olly Murray knew that something was seriously wrong with her family. Starting with her first pregnancy in the late 1950s, she suffered from strange, unexplained symptoms—painful body aches and fatigue, bizarre rashes, headaches, joint pain, and fevers. The list of symptoms was so long and perplexing that she started bringing it to every doctor appointment. Over the years, her husband and three children experienced similar problems.

SIZE: 1/16 in (2 mm) (nymphs are smaller—about the size of a flake of pepper)

FAMILY: Ixodidae

HABITAT: Woods and forests

DISTRIBUTION: East Coast, found as far south as Florida and as far west as Minnesota, Iowa, and Texas; Ixodes pacificus in Washington, Oregon, and California, with limited distribution in neighboring states

MEET THE RELATIVES: There are roughly 900 species of ticks worldwide.

The doctors in Murray's hometown of Lyme, Connecticut, never had any answers. Her family members tested negative for everything from lupus to seasonal allergies. As far as the doctors could tell, there was nothing medically wrong with them. A few doctors recommended psychiatric treatment, and some suggested penicillin or aspirin. Based on the information they had, there was nothing else they could do.

In 1975, everything changed. Armed with the knowledge that a few of her neighbors had similar problems—and that several local children had been diagnosed with a rare juvenile form of rheumatoid arthritis—Murray called an epidemiologist at the state health department. He took down the information but had no solutions.

A month later, Murray was surprised that a young doctor named Allen Steere was waiting for her at a doctor's appointment at Yale. The state epidemiologist that Murray had called the month before had contacted Steere afterward to tell him about the cluster of juvenile rheumatoid arthritis cases in Lyme. Steere listened to Murray's entire story and began an investigation that led to the discovery of a previously unknown tick-transmitted disease. Although the civic leaders were not thrilled by the idea of having a dreadful malady named after their town, the scientists called it Lyme disease—and the name stuck.

Although the civic leaders were not thrilled by the idea of having a dreadful malady named after their town, the scientists called it Lyme disease—and the name stuck.

The deer tick, also called the blacklegged tick, lives in heavily populated areas along the East Coast. It is responsible for most of the cases of Lyme disease in the United States. Its ability to transmit the disease depends in part on its strange life cycle, which can involve three different hosts as it matures through three life stages. When the larvae first emerge from eggs in the fall, they feed on rats, mice, or birds. They spend the winter on the forest floor, and in the spring, they molt into the second life stage, the nympha stage, and feed again—this time on a small rodent or a human. By late summer, the nymphs have become adults that feed on large animals, primarily deer, for the last year or so of their lives.

When the ticks are in the larvae stage, they sometimes take the bacteria that cause Lyme disease into their bodies during their first meal. When that happens, they are capable of transmitting the bacteria the next time they feed in the nymph stage. Despite the name "deer tick," the deer themselves don't become infected with Lyme disease. But they do help move the ticks around and bring tick populations into close contact with people.

Lyme disease is nothing new. Medical writings dating back as far as 1550 BCE referred to "tick fever," and European doctors had been investigating symptoms similar to those caused by Lyme disease throughout the nineteenth century. (In Europe, the disease is transmitted by the tick *Ixodes ricinus*, called the castor bean tick for its resemblance to the poisonous seed.) Today, it is the most frequently reported vector-borne illness in the United States, with twenty-five to thirty thousand new infections reported each year.

If the disease is detected soon after a person is exposed, antibiotics can be effective. The treatments for long-term infections can be more complicated and difficult. Doctors advise avoiding ticks altogether, using insect repellents, wearing protective clothing, and closely examining the body for ticks every day so that they can be removed quickly before transmission takes place. People who live in tick-infested areas know to watch for the telltale bulls-eye rash that is a sign that a person has Lyme disease. Called erythema migrans, it often occurs at the site of an infected tick bite within the first month of infection.

It is now known that a species of tick on the West Coast, *Ixodes pacificus*, also transmits Lyme disease. Other ticks in the United States transmit a variety of illnesses, including Rocky Mountain spotted fever, southern tick-associated rash illness, and tularemia, a disease that causes swollen lymph glands, sores and ulcers, and pneumonia.

BED BUG
Cimex lectularius

In Toronto, a sixty-year-old man went to his doctor complaining of fatigue. The doctor found severe anemia, which occurs due to a lack of iron in the blood, so he treated the man with a prescription dose of iron. A month later, the man was back with even worse symptoms, requiring a transfusion of someone's donated blood to replenish his own before he could return home. A few weeks later, he needed another transfusion. The blood loss was inexplicable and frightening.

SIZE: 3/16 in (4–5 mm)

FAMILY: Cimicidae

HABITAT: Nests, caves, and other warm, dry places near food sources

DISTRIBUTION: Temperate regions throughout the world

MEET THE RELATIVES: The Cimicidae family includes not only bed bugs but bat bugs and bird bugs as well. All depend on the blood of their prey for survival.

Then the doctor paid a call to his patient at home. The problem was obvious: bed bugs were everywhere. He could even see them crawling on the man during the visit. The public health department was called in. After the apartment was sprayed with insecticide and his old furniture removed, the man gradually recovered.

The bed bug travels at night, lurking in low light, feeling its way toward warmth and the tantalizing odor of carbon dioxide. It approaches its dinner—in other words, *you*—with outstretched antennae, gripping the skin tightly with its tiny claws. Once it has a good grip, it begins rocking back and forth, working needlelike feeding organs called stylets into the skin. It bites gently, piercing the skin just enough to get the blood flowing. The stylets probe around under the skin in search of a good-sized blood vessel to tap into. Its saliva contains an anticoagulant, an ingredient that prevents clotting, so the bug can settle down to feed. If it is left alone to enjoy its meal, it will feed for about five minutes and then wander off. But if you were to swat at the bug in your sleep, it would probably move a short distance away and bite again, leading to a telltale series of three sequential puncture wounds. Doctors call these bites "breakfast, lunch, and dinner."

Doctors call these bites "breakfast, lunch, and dinner."

Before World War II, bed bugs were a fact of life in the United States and throughout the world. Pesticides developed around that time helped eliminate them, but now the bloodsucking parasite is back. One of the reasons for the bug's reappearance is an increase in international travel. In addition, people are less likely to routinely spray pesticides in homes, offices, and hotels. Targeted baits are more common now. Most alarmingly, bed bugs have developed a resistance to chemical controls.

What has this meant for the average New Yorker? Although bed bugs have not been shown to transmit disease, the bites can cause allergic reactions, swelling, rashes, and secondary infections from scratching. The blood loss from a severe infestation could be serious enough to cause anemia, particularly in children and people in poor health. The sleep loss and emotional distress alone are enough to bring on serious psychological problems.

A bed bug can survive up to a year without feeding. In the wild, it may live in a nest or cave alongside its prey. In the city, it prefers upholstery, loose wallpaper, or the dry, dark spaces behind pictures or inside light sockets. The most severe outbreaks may be accompanied by streaks of feces along the tufts of upholstery. A strange sweet odor that comes from the bug's scent glands pervades homes with large populations of the bugs. The compounds it produces, hexanol and octenol, are used to communicate with other bed bugs, but the smell is a giveaway that trained dogs can detect even when people can't. It's been described as smelling like coriander—and in fact, the name *coriander* comes from the word *koris*, which in Greek means "bug."

Controlling bed bugs is not easy, especially in apartment buildings, where they can move from one room to another via ductwork (tubes that carry hot or cold air throughout the home) or even cracks in the plaster. City dwellers are starting to avoid used furniture for fear of picking up unwanted hitchhikers. Mattress companies have learned the hard way not to use the same truck to haul away old mattresses and deliver new ones, because bed bugs can be spread to new mattresses that way.

One promising new control is an insecticide dust mixed with the bugs' own pheromones. This so-called alarm pheromone entices them to get up and move around, exposing them to enough of the insecticide to cause them to simply dry up and die. An even more natural form of pest control may show up all by itself: the house centipede, *Scutigera coleoptrata*, feeds on bed bugs, as does the so-called masked hunter, *Reduvius personatus*, an assassin bug that gets its blood meal by robbing bed bugs of theirs.

BODY LICE
Pediculus humanus humanus
(also known as Pediculus humanus corporis)

eneral Napoleon Bonaparte of France marched into Russia with over half a million men in 1812 and left, defeated, with only a few thousand. What happened? Napoleon blamed the cold winter, but scientists now know that it was a tiny, wingless, flattened insect that brought the world's mightiest army to its knees. During their march, the

SIZE: $\frac{1}{16}$–$\frac{1}{8}$ in (2–3 mm)

FAMILY: Pediculidae

HABITAT: Clothing and human skin

DISTRIBUTION: Worldwide from tropical regions to the Arctic Circle

MEET THE RELATIVES: Body lice are closely related to head lice, which also feed on human blood.

soldiers were forced to scrounge food and shelter from peasants in the Polish and Russian countryside, and from those impoverished people they picked up a nasty case of body lice. One soldier wrote that he awoke to a sensation of "unbearable tingling . . . and to my horror discovered that I was covered with vermin!" He jumped up and threw his clothes into the fire, a move he surely came to regret as winter approached and supplies grew scarce.

But it wasn't just the "unbearable tingling" that led to Napoleon's defeat. Body lice carry typhus, trench fever, and any number of other nasty diseases that can decimate an army. Napoleon's few surviving troops were so sick that they had no choice but to retreat from Russia, a defeat that marked the beginning of the end of his brilliant military career.

In 1919, at the height of the Russian Civil War, typhus was again rampant as a result of the poverty, crowded conditions, and warfare that breed body lice, causing Lenin to say that "Either socialism will defeat the louse, or the louse will defeat socialism."

Body lice are, fortunately, unfamiliar to most people. The creatures have evolved to lay eggs in the seams and linings of clothing, not on the body itself. For this reason,

In the most severe cases, up to thirty thousand body lice have been reported on one individual.

they're found only among homeless or impoverished people who must wear the same clothes for weeks at a time without washing. The eggs hatch in response to body heat, so clothes that are worn constantly provide the best breeding ground. The newly emerged nymphs migrate to the skin and must feed within a few hours to survive. Over the next week, they grow into a full adult and live for a few weeks more, feeding on human blood the whole time. In the most severe cases, up to thirty thousand body lice have been reported on one individual. Even without the possibility of disease transmission, simply being plagued by these tiny bloodsuckers can be dangerous.

Serious infestations cause a strange thickening and discoloration of the skin known as vagabond disease, or pediculosis corporis. People also develop swollen lymph nodes, fever, rash, headache, joint and muscle pain, and allergies, simply from exposure to the lice. Once a person develops a high temperature, the lice will leave them and look for another, less overheated, human host, increasing the likelihood of spreading disease.

One of the most common louse-borne diseases is typhus, which is caused by infection with bacteria that also live in the blood of flying squirrels. The bacteria aren't actually transmitted by the louse's bite. Instead, they are excreted in lice feces, which make their way into the bloodstream when people scratch their bites and inadvertently push the bacteria into the bite wound. Because the bacteria remain viable in lice feces for ninety days, opportunities for infection are plentiful. The disease causes fever, chills, rashes, and eventually delirium, coma, and perhaps death.

About 20 percent of typhus cases are fatal, although death rates have been much higher during times of war. Even the survivors live with the bacteria in their lymph nodes for years. (Today's modern antibiotics offer a full recovery.) While humans may survive a bout of typhus, the louse never does. The man who developed the typhus vaccine, Hans Zinsser, wrote that "If lice can dread, the nightmare of their lives is the fear of some day of inhabiting an infected . . . human . . . To the louse, *we* are the dreaded emissaries of death."

In addition to plaguing soldiers living in crowded, unhygienic conditions, the disease also spread to Native Americans after European contact in the 1500s, killing millions. Today, typhus outbreaks still occur, primarily in refugee camps, slums, and other areas of mass migrations, severe crowding, and poverty.

Lice were once thought to emerge naturally from the skin, as if born from humans. It wasn't until 1882 that Dr. L. D. Bulkley put this myth to rest, writing that "All the fabulous stories in regard to lice issuing from abscesses or sores are utterly without scientific foundation—are, indeed, impossibly absurd."

HEAD LICE
Pediculus humanus capitis

Head lice date back seven million years, when humans and chimpanzees shared a common ancestor. Because lice have the strange ability to match the color of the skin on which they hatch, an infestation of head lice can be hard to detect—an unpleasant surprise, but not a particularly dangerous one. Head lice do not transmit disease. Their presence is not even a sign of uncleanliness. But head lice are infuriatingly difficult to get rid of and surprisingly common—second only to the common cold in communicable diseases that afflict schoolchildren. An estimated six to twelve million children are infested every year, or about a quarter of all children in the United States.

SIZE: $1/16$–$1/8$ in (2–3 mm)
FAMILY: Pediculidae
HABITAT: Human scalps, especially around ears and at the neckline
DISTRIBUTION: Worldwide
MEET THE RELATIVES: Body lice evolved from head lice about 107,000 years ago, around the time humans started wearing clothing.

Female head lice lay their eggs, called nits, along a strand of hair, excreting a little cement to secure them in place. (In fact, a female louse risks accidentally gluing herself down as well.) They prefer to deposit their young around the ears or the neck, and this is where they can be most easily seen. Although special medicated

But head lice are infuriatingly difficult to get rid of and surprisingly common—second only to the common cold in communicable diseases that afflict schoolchildren. shampoos can kill lice, in some parts of the country, the lice are growing resistant to those chemicals. A new generation of prescription creams and shampoos are available, but many parents resort to the old-fashioned approach of running a fine comb through wet hair coated in vegetable oil to remove the nits, one at a time.

THE ENEMY WITHIN

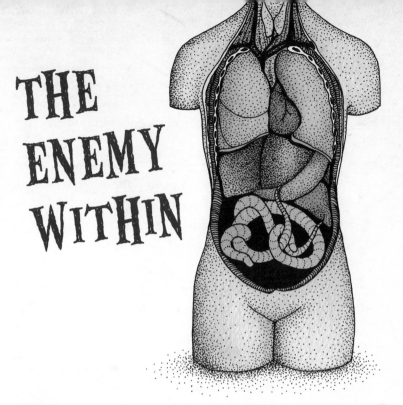

German physician Friedrich Küchenmeister published a book in 1857 on human parasites in which he described the distress people find themselves in when they discover tapeworms attempting to leave their bodies. "The passage of the segments without feces is a constant annoyance to the patient," he wrote. "The proglottids [tapeworm segments] adhering to the naked body in the trousers, or under the petticoats, being disagreeable, from their clammy coldness, disturb the patients greatly; and women especially are afraid lest the proglottids should fall unperceived upon the ground when they are walking or standing."

But parasitic worms do more than embarrass ladies in petticoats. And often, they do it with the help of some other creature that plays a critical role in getting the worm into our bodies.

GUINEA WORM *Dracunculus medinensis:* Dracunculiasis, more commonly known as guinea worm disease, is an ancient affliction that has been found in Egyptian mummies. It is transmitted by a tiny freshwater crustacean called a copepod that people swallow when they drink from ponds or other unclean water sources. Once they swallow it, the copepod dies but the guinea worms inhabiting it move into the small intestine to grow and mate. The male dies, but the female eventually reaches two to three feet (sixty to ninety centimeters) in length, resembling a long strand of spaghetti. She burrows into connective tissue, around joints, or alongside the bones of the arms and legs.

Guinea worm disease, is an ancient affliction that has been found in Egyptian mummies.

People may not know they have been infested until after a year. At that point, the female decides she is ready to leave and moves near the skin, creating blisters that rupture after a few days. Soaking the wound in cool water brings some relief from the burning pain—which is exactly what the worm is counting on! As soon as her victim dips an arm or leg in the water, she emerges slightly from the skin and releases millions of larvae. And the life cycle continues. Worst of all, she takes her time exiting the body. Any attempts to grab her or cut her into pieces will only result in the worm retreating back into her hole and emerging later somewhere else.

Treating people who have the disease is not easy, as there is no medication that works against the worm. Instead, people have to wait for the parasite to show herself, then wrap a piece of gauze or tie a stick around the bit that emerges from the skin so that she cannot retreat. Every day, inch by inch, the visible part of the worm is wrapped up until, after about a month, she has slithered out entirely.

The fight against guinea worm disease, led by President Jimmy Carter's foundation, has been remarkably effective. There were 3.5 million cases in twenty countries throughout Africa and Asia in 1986. By 2015, only twenty-two cases remained worldwide. To stop the disease, people filter their water through mesh cloths. If current efforts to fight the parasite continue, guinea worm disease will become the first parasitic disease to be eliminated completely, and the first human disease of any kind to be wiped out without any assistance from vaccines or medications.

LYMPHATIC FILARIASIS *Wuchereria bancrofti* and *Brugia malayi:* Also known as elephantiasis, infestation with these parasitic worms causes thick, wrinkled skin and grotesque swelling of arms, legs, breasts, or genitals. Over 120 million people worldwide carry the parasite, with forty million suffering the most severe symptoms. The infant worms are called microfilariae. They can develop into larvae only while inside a mosquito, and those larvae can reach adulthood only inside a human.

One bite from an infected mosquito probably won't transmit the disease. In fact, it can take hundreds of bites for enough male and female larvae to enter a person's body, track each other down, and reproduce. Once established, however, the adult worms settle into the lymph system and build nest-like structures that block lymphatic fluid and cause the characteristic swelling. Adults live for five to seven years, mating and producing millions of offspring. The offspring circulate in the blood, hoping a mosquito will bite the human in which they live to continue their life cycle.

This disease is found in the poorest parts of the world, including Africa, South America, parts of South Asia, the Pacific, and the Caribbean. Although a blood test can detect the presence of the microfilariae, the tiny creatures circulate through the bloodstream only at night when mosquitoes are biting. During the day, they may not show up on a blood test at all. And treatment is even harder. There is no way to eliminate the adult worms, but an annual deworming pill called Mectizan will kill their offspring and stop further transmission of the disease.

But annual pill distributions are not easy in remote areas, or in countries torn apart by violence. Now public health officials are trying a new approach—adding the dewormer to table salt, at a cost of only twenty-six cents per bag. In China, the disease was eliminated after the government ordered people to use the salt. Dewormers kill several other annoying parasites, including roundworms, lice, and scabies.

PORK TAPEWORM *Taenia solium:* In the fall of 2008, a thirty-seven-year-old Arizona woman was in for the most frightening day of her life. She was being wheeled into surgery to have a tumor removed from deep inside her brain. It was a risky procedure, but she had little choice: her left arm was numb, she had lost her balance, and she was beginning to have difficulty swallowing. The tumor had to come out.

With her skull open and her brain exposed, the surgeon started laughing. He was relieved to find out that, rather than an intractable tumor, the woman had been suffering from tapeworms. Removing the worm was a simple, and the woman awoke from surgery to the news that she didn't have a brain tumor after all.

An infestation of pork tapeworm begins when a person eats raw or undercooked pork loaded with tapeworm larvae. Inside pigs, the larvae form fluid-filled cysts that don't develop into adults unless they are eaten by humans. Once a person eats pork infested with those cysts, the larvae settle into the wall of the intestines, where they mature and reach several meters in length. Adult tapeworms can occupy the intestines for twenty years, releasing thousands of eggs that get discharged from the body through feces. The adult tapeworm may exit the body on its own, or it can be killed with prescription medication.

The Arizona woman was most likely infected through contact with feces impregnated with tapeworm eggs—not through under-cooked pork. One way this could happen is if restaurant kitchen workers are infested with tapeworms and don't wash after going to the bathroom. The tapeworm eggs from contact with feces remain on their hands, and then they prepare food. When people swallow the eggs rather than the larvae, a different kind of infestation occurs. The eggs, once swallowed, hatch into larvae that are initially far more mobile, preferring to explore the body rather than remain in the intestines. They can migrate to the lungs, the liver, or the brain.

Although pigs serve as hosts for tapeworms, allowing the eggs to develop into larvae, humans are the only known "definitive host." That means that larvae can reach adulthood only in a human.

Experts estimate that pork tapeworms infest one in ten people worldwide. The rate is much higher in impoverished countries. Tapeworms can cause severe digestive problems, anemia, and organ damage, and may cause people to gain weight. The presence of tapeworms in the brain is now the leading cause of epilepsy world-wide—a tragedy that can easily be prevented with better sanitation.

ROUNDWORM *Ascaris lumbricoides:* Roundworms do not need help from a mosquito or a snail to find their way into the human digestive tract. At over a foot (thirty centimeters) long, and roughly the diameter of a pencil, they are perfectly capable of taking care of themselves. Roundworms settle into the small intestine, below the stomach. They live there for up to two years. Females can lay up to two hundred thousand eggs per day. Those eggs pass from the body in the feces. Once on the ground, they develop into tiny larvae that may find their way back into the human body. This is more likely to happen in areas with poor sanitation, where children may play on the ground near areas used as a latrine. It is also common in communities that use improperly treated human waste for fertilizer on crops that people then eat without proper washing.

Once back inside the body, the larvae spend about two weeks in the lungs, then move into the throat, where they are swallowed so that they can reach the small intestine and grow into an adult. In the worst cases, people may harbor several hundred adult roundworms in their intestines. Oddly, the worms are greatly troubled by general anesthesia, used to make patients unconscious before surgery. Roundworms have been known to flee the body via the nose or mouth on the operating table.

Although some people experience only mild abdominal symptoms, a serious case of roundworm infestation (called ascariasis) can lead to respiratory problems, nutritional deficiencies, organ damage, and severe allergic reactions. An estimated 1.5 billion people—up to one-quarter of the world's population—are infested with roundworms. Most of those are children. Roundworm kills an estimated sixty thousand people per year, mainly through intestinal blockages that cause the digestive system to stop working properly. It is found in tropical and subtropical regions around the world and sometimes occurs in southern regions of the United States. Prescription medications can kill the worms, but improved sanitation is the only sure way to eliminate it.

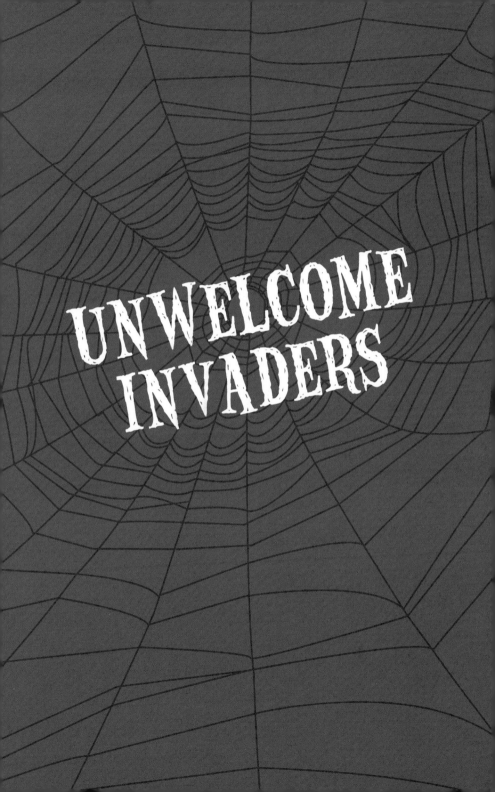

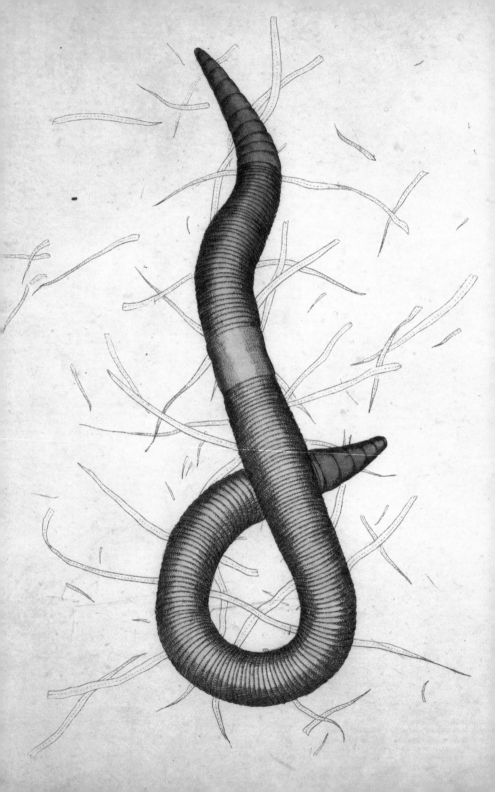

NIGHTCRAWLER
Lumbricus terrestris

By the 1990s, forest scientists at the University of Minnesota knew that strange changes had occurred in their forests. Something was happening, people said. The young understory plants that grow on the forest floor—the

SIZE: 10 in (25 cm) in length
FAMILY: Lumbricidae
HABITAT: Rich, moist soils
DISTRIBUTION: Worldwide
MEET THE RELATIVES: The red worm, *L. rubellus*, is often found in compost piles, as is the red wiggler *Eisenia fetida*.

ferns and wildflowers—were disappearing. There were fewer trees, and almost no young trees. When the snow melted in spring, there was only bare dirt between the trees, not the carpet of greenery people expected to see. It was as if the forest had stopped renewing itself. The scientists were puzzled.

Then one of the researchers, Cindy Hale, read an article about the forests in New York. "It mentioned, in a kind of an offhand way, that increases in earthworm populations might be causing changes in understory plants," she said. "That's when it finally occurred to us to go out into the forest with a shovel and dig."

What they found was earthworms. This shouldn't be cause for alarm—after all, earthworms are good for the soil. They improve drainage, they move nutrients around, they deposit their rich worm poop around plant roots, and they help break down organic matter.

Farmers and gardeners brag about their earthworm populations as indicators of healthy soil. But as the Minnesota team was about to find out, earthworms are not always as beneficial as people believe.

Many of the worms they dug up—also the largest and easiest to identify—turned out to be a European species. *Lumbricus terrestris*, better known as the nightcrawler, was the largest and easiest to identify. *Lumbricus rubellus*, a smaller species sometimes called a red worm, was also abundant in the soil. They went on to find more than a dozen nonnative species living in the forest floor.

Earthworms are not always as beneficial as people believe.

Because Minnesota was covered by glaciers during the last Ice Age, about eleven thousand years ago, its forests have evolved without any native earthworms at all. Native North American worms can be found throughout much of the country, but those northernmost portions were absolutely free of worms—until European species arrived.

European worms came to the United States with settlers in potted plants, in soil used as a ship's ballast to provide stability, and embedded in wagon wheels and the hooves of cattle. They moved across the country as quickly as the settlers themselves did. Today, the earthworm population in a typical American backyard is likely to be made up primarily of European worms. In most gardens, these worms do only good—but that was not the case in Minnesota.

It took several years of study to prove that European worms were radically transforming the forest. By monitoring test plots, Hale and her team were able to demonstrate that European worms could completely devour the layer of leaves that fell every autumn. Under normal circumstances, the leaves would remain on the ground year after year, forming a spongy duff layer that native plants required to germinate and grow. But rotten leaves are like candy to the night-crawler. In areas with the heaviest infestation, the duff layer was gone entirely and replaced by a thin blanket of earthworm castings. The native Minnesota trees and wildflowers simply couldn't survive without the duff layer.

And as people come into the forests around the Great Lakes, bringing with them live worms for fishing bait, soil for fill dirt, or even tires caked in mud, the earthworms continue to spread. Even building a golf course near a forest can pose a risk, as acres and acres of sod are installed, complete with whatever species of earthworms may have been living in it.

What can be done to stop the invasion of European worms into those northern forests that evolved without them? They can't be evicted—it's not possible to put up a fence to keep earthworms out. Hale and her team found that keeping deer out of the forest can make a difference, because whatever understory plants manage to survive in the earthworm-rich soil often get eaten by deer. They hope to slow the spread of the worms by discouraging the use of worms as fishing bait and by educating people about the potential hazards of the gardener's best friend.

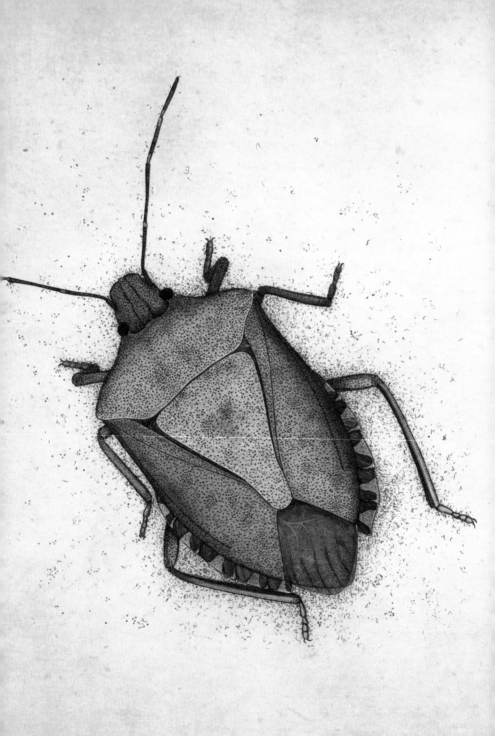

BROWN MARMORATED STINK BUG

Halyomorpha halys

S ome residents of Pennsylvania and New Jersey dread the arrival of autumn, because it means the beginning of the annual invasion of flattened, grayish-brown insects from China. They crawl in the tiniest crevice, able to gain entry through cracks around doors and windows, crevices

SIZE: 11/16 in (1.7 cm)

FAMILY: Pentatomidae

HABITAT: Orchards, agricultural fields, meadows

DISTRIBUTION: China, Japan, Taiwan, Korea, and parts of the United States

MEET THE RELATIVES: Stink bugs are a large and diverse family found in Australia, North America, Europe, Asia, Africa, and South America. Relations include the leaf-footed bugs, which feed on a wide variety of plants.

in the attic, and ductwork. They make themselves at home, glad to be away from the winter's chill and ready to spend the next several months enjoying indoor life.

Members of a family in Lower Allen Township, Pennsylvania, complained that when they opened kitchen cabinets, the bugs were sitting in their dishes. They found them waiting inside drawers and under the bed, and crawling through the attic by the hundreds. And when Christmas came, the bugs climbed up the family's tree and sat among the ornaments.

The husband couldn't stand the sight of the bugs. When he found them in his barbecue grill, he cleaned the entire grill to scrub away even the memory of them. His actions proved pointless, though—a couple dozen bugs returned just a few minutes later. He stretched duct tape around his windows, but the bugs kept coming back. Going to work didn't give him a break, either. As a mailman, he found them in mailboxes all day long. "I'm starting to see them everywhere," he told reporters. It was an entomophobe's worst nightmare.

What makes these home invaders so intolerable is their smell. It is difficult to describe the odor of a stink bug. Some people characterize it as a rotten fruit smell, a combination of cherries and grass, or a moldy, musty almond fragrance. Most people simply call it a foul, heinous odor that they'll never forget. Disturbing the bugs, stepping on them, or vacuuming them up—the control method recommended by experts—releases the stink. That stink can be a signal that attracts more stink bugs to the home. Light also attracts stink bugs, and in large quantities, they have even created traffic hazards. In 1905, Phoenix residents often traveled via streetcar. When the city installed electrical streetlights, they drew so many stink bugs to intersections that the streetcars couldn't plough through the piles of bugs massed on the ground.

The brown marmorated stink bug was probably introduced in Allentown, Pennsylvania, by accident in the late 1990s. Like other stink bugs or shield bugs, these wide, flat bugs look like a shield when viewed from above. Their defensive secretions have a bitter almond smell. The emissions contain cyanide, which is found in certain foods, such as almonds, and can be poisonous in some circumstances. And while stink bugs are generally harmless, inflicting only minimal damage to plants, this Asian invader is being watched closely as it has the potential to become a pest to fruit trees, soybeans, and other crops. After establishing itself in Pennsylvania, it moved into New Jersey and then showed up across the country in Oregon. It has now been seen in twenty-seven states.

The stink bug is universally despised as an indoor pest. It crawls around in closets, requiring people to shake out their clothes before getting dressed. Women find the bugs crawling in their hair. They creep in through window-mounted air conditioning units. While insecticides sprayed around a home's exterior may keep the bugs out, they are of little use against the bugs indoors and may pose more health hazards than the bugs themselves. Vacuuming up the bugs does work, but the stink is so powerful that most people buy a separate vacuum cleaner just for bug removal.

When they opened kitchen cabinets, the bugs were sitting in their dishes.

The bugs don't breed in the winter, so they don't start new families indoors. Once spring arrives, the adults leave on their own to return to gardens and fields, where they will mate and lay eggs. The eggs hatch in late summer, and the newborn nymphs go through five stages of molting until emerging as adults in late August. This new generation then goes in search of a place to spend the winter, settling indoors by October, just as their parents did.

AFRICAN BAT BUG

Afrocimex constrictus

W hen members of a North Carolina family discovered tiny, bloodsucking parasites in their home, they had no idea that there was worse news still to come. The bugs were a sign that bats were living in the attic. They were bat bugs, parasites that prefer bats but will seek out other warm-blooded creatures when they get exceedingly hungry. An adult bat bug can survive on one blood meal per year, so they don't need to eat often. But to have the energy to reproduce, they dine repeatedly on the blood of live bats. The bugs don't live on the bats themselves. They hide in the warm, dry crevices of an attic or a hollow tree where bats also dwell, and they eat when the bats come home to roost in the early morning hours.

SIZE: 3/16 in (5 mm)

FAMILY: Cimicidae

HABITAT: Close proximity to bat colonies, usually trees or caves, sometimes the eaves and attics of houses

DISTRIBUTION: East Africa, with other species found worldwide, including the U.S. Midwest

MEET THE RELATIVES: The bat bug is closely related to bed bugs and a few other insects that feed on the blood of warm-blooded animals.

Alarmed by the presence of these bugs and the bats they feed on, the family contacted an exterminator, who advised waiting until fall, when the young bats would be old enough to fly out of

Once their hosts have left, bat bugs will wander the house and feed on humans.

the attic on their own. Then the cracks and crevices around the roof could be patched while the bats were away. Using this method, the family eventually succeeded in ridding the home of bats. Unfortunately, the bat bugs were not so easily evicted.

Once their hosts have left, bat bugs will wander the house and feed on humans. For humans, signs of an infestation include flesh-colored welts on the skin, often in groups of two or three, and itching. The bites are generally harmless, although they could become inflamed or infected from too much scratching. The bugs themselves are rarely spotted as they typically feed while the host is sleeping. At only one-eighth of an inch (three millimeters) long, oval-shaped, and dark red in color, they are almost indistinguishable from their close relative, the bed bug.

MILLIPEDE
Tachypodoiulus niger, *others*

In general, a millipede is not a particularly threatening creature. Unlike centipedes, which actively hunt for prey and inject their victims with venom to subdue them, millipedes creep slowly along the ground, scavenging for dead leaves. They are called detritivores because they sift through the rotting material left at the base of plants and break it

SIZE: Up to 2⁵/₁₆ in (6 cm)

FAMILY: Julidae

HABITAT: Leaf litter and forest floor where decaying vegetation is abundant

DISTRIBUTION: Throughout Europe, particularly in Great Britain, Ireland, and Germany

MEET THE RELATIVES: There are about ten thousand known species of millipedes, including the giant African millipede *Archispirostreptus gigas*, which reaches 11 in (28 cm) in length and lives up to ten years in captivity, and the tiny pill millipede.

down further to help the cycle of natural composting continue. When attacked, most millipedes just curl into a ball and hope their tough body armor protects them. So what's not to like about these peace-loving vegetarian recyclers?

Their sheer numbers, for one thing. Millipede invasions are not only creepy—they're destructive. Stories of millipedes swarming over railroad tracks have been in the news since the advent of the railroad, but some of the more recent accounts are truly astonishing.

Monkeys in Venezuela search for a four-inch-long (ten centimeters) millipede called *Orthoporus dorsovittatus* so that they can rub the millipedes into their fur and use their secretions to keep mosquitoes away.

Express trains outside Tokyo were brought to a halt in 2000 when the creatures swarmed over the tracks. Their crushed bodies created a wet, squishy mess that made the wheels slip. In Australia, the same thing happened—nonnative Portuguese millipedes, *Ommatoiulus moreletii*, infested rail lines, forcing the delay or cancellation of trains that simply couldn't gain traction on the slippery tracks.

The situation is even worse in parts of Scotland. The European black millipede *Tachypodoiulus niger* is such a nuisance there that residents of three remote villages in the Highlands have been forced to resort to nighttime blackouts to keep the millipedes, which are attracted to light, from creeping into their homes at night and massing around bathrooms and kitchens. A local postmistress told reporters, "They are horrible. They start in April and last year they were still coming in October. It's hard to believe how bad it gets unless you are here and see them."

A town in Bavaria tried the blackout strategy, but gave up and eventually built a wall around the town to keep millipedes out. The wall, which surrounds the town of Obereichstaett, is made of slick metal with a lip that the creatures can't cross. (Australians have used something similar for years to keep millipedes out of their houses.) One resident of the town said that before the wall went up, he couldn't walk down the street without crushing dozens of them. The smell alone was unbearable.

Millipedes, which have two pairs of legs per segment, produce a number of unpleasant compounds as a defense mechanism. Some species release hydrogen cyanide, a toxic gas that they formulate in a specialized reaction chamber if attacked. This gas is so strong that other creatures placed in a glass jar with these millipedes will surely die. The species *Glomeris marginata* produces a chemical compound that it uses to sedate wolf spiders when attacked.

These defensive chemicals are rarely harmful to humans. A person would have to deliberately cover themselves with the secretions of a millipede to experience a rash or burn from them. In fact, one animal actually does this. Monkeys in Venezuela search for a four–inch-long (ten centimeters) millipede called *Orthoporus dorsovittatus* so that they can rub the millipedes into their fur and use their secretions to keep mosquitoes away.

ZOMBIES

The insect world has its own version of *The Walking Dead*. These bugs don't just eat other bugs—they actually inhabit them and force them to do harm on their behalf. Some victims are made to jump in a lake, while others find themselves defending their captors against other attackers. Rarely, however, do the "zombies" benefit from this strange behavior. Once their role in their predator's life cycle is over, they go from being "undead" to simply "dead."

EMERALD COCKROACH WASP *Ampulex compressa:* Also called a jewel wasp for its peacock-green iridescent coloring, this diminutive wasp is not afraid to tackle a much larger cockroach and force it to do what it wants. When the female wasp is pregnant, she hunts down a cockroach and delivers a sting that briefly renders it immobile. She then delivers another sting directly into the roach's brain that disables its instinct to flee. Once she has gained control of the cockroach, the wasp can lead it around by its antennae like a dog on a leash.

The roach follows the wasp into her nest and sits down obediently. The wasp lays an egg on the roach's abdomen and leaves it in the nest, where it will wait patiently for the egg to hatch into a larva. The larva chews a hole in the roach's abdomen and crawls inside, spending the next week eating its internal organs and constructing a cocoon. This eventually kills the roach, but the cocoon remains in its body for a month; a full-grown adult then emerges from the cockroach's body, leaving the shell of the roach behind.

GREEN-BANDED BROODSAC *Leucochloridium paradoxum:* In what is surely one of nature's most bizarre life cycles, this flatworm's eggs are excreted in bird droppings, where they must be eaten by snails to hatch. Once devoured, they move into the snail's digestive tract and emerge to form long tubelike structures that invade the snail's tentacles. At that point, the snail cannot see or retract its tentacles. The tentacles, once invaded by this parasite, turn bright colors and wave around in the open, a behavior that is very attractive to birds. The birds swoop down and take a bite, which is exactly what the parasite wants. Only when it is safely inside the body of a bird can it grow into adulthood and lay eggs, which are excreted in the bird's droppings so that the cycle can begin again.

HAIRWORM *Spinochordodes tellinii:* This parasitic worm begins its life as a microscopic larva, swimming around in water where it is swallowed by a grasshopper taking a drink. Once inside the grasshopper, it grows into adulthood, but it has a problem—it needs to get back into the water to find a mate. To accomplish this, it takes control of the grasshopper's brain—perhaps by releasing a protein that alters the insect's central nervous system—and convinces its host to commit suicide by jumping into the nearest body of water. Once the grasshopper has drowned, the hairworm leaves the body and swims away.

PHORID FLY *Pseudacteon spp.:* A tiny South American fly may be the solution to the fire ant problem in the American South. This fly injects its eggs into the fire ant. The larvae eat the ant's brains, causing the ant to wander aimlessly around for a week or two. Eventually, the ant's head falls off and the adult flies emerge in search of more fire ants to kill. This violent and vicious approach to pest control is deeply satisfying to people who have been plagued by the ants.

TONGUE-EATING LOUSE *Cymothoa exigua:* An aquatic crustacean resembling a pill bug, this creature enters the body of a fish through its gills and latches onto its tongue. It feeds on the fish's tongue until there is nothing left but a stub. This doesn't bother the louse—it holds on to the stub, continuing to drink blood from it, and acts as a tongue so that the fish can continue to eat. From time to time, the parasites are found inside the mouths of whole snapper in fish markets, much to the horror of shoppers.

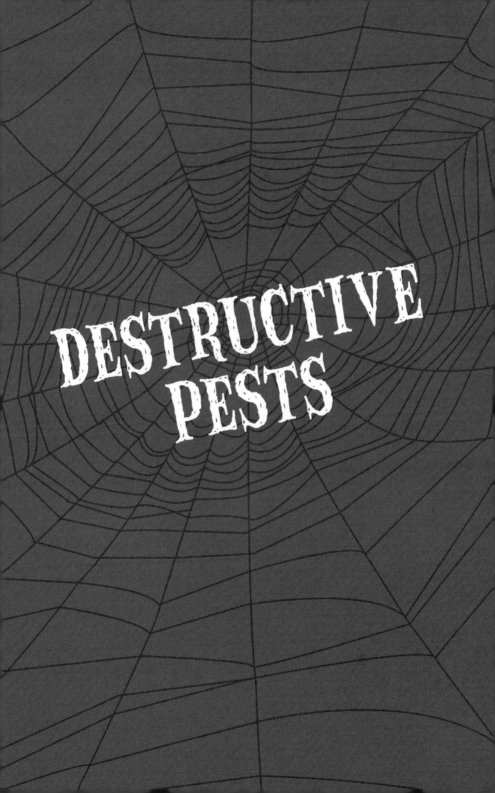

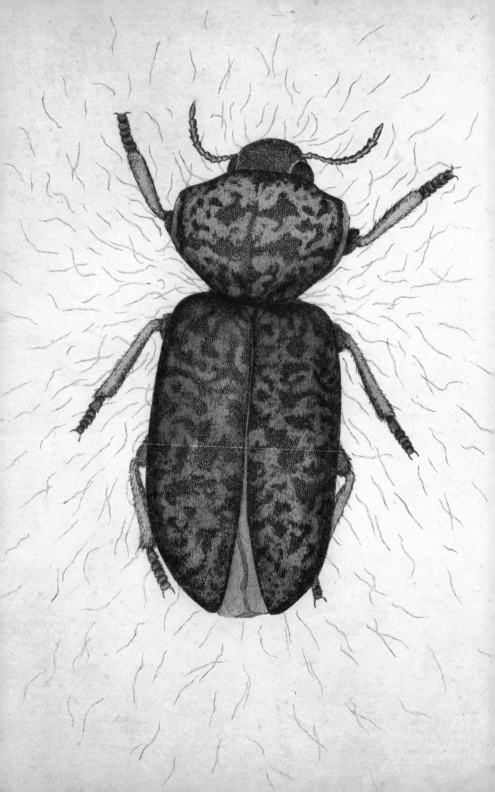

DEATH-WATCH BEETLE
Xestobium rufovillosum

"**N**ow, I say, there came to my ears a low, dull, quick sound, such as a watch makes when enveloped in cotton. I knew that sound well, too. It was the beating of the old man's heart."

So says the madman who narrates Edgar Allan Poe's frightful story "The Tell-Tale Heart." He describes his victim groaning in the night as he hears the approach of death. And what was the sound that kept the old man—and his murderer—awake at night? "He was still sitting up in the bed listening;—just as I have done, night after night, hearkening to the death watches in the wall."

The death-watch beetle to which Poe referred is a bug that sits in the rafters of old homes, quietly munching away at the beams and calling to its mate with the soft *tick-tick* sound it makes by tapping its head against the wood.

SIZE: $1/4$ in (7 mm)

FAMILY: Anobiidae

HABITAT: Decaying wood in forests, or in the timbers of old buildings

DISTRIBUTION: In England, with its relatives scattered across Europe, North America, and Australia

MEET THE RELATIVES: The cigarette beetle *Lasioderma serricorne*, the drugstore beetle *Stegobium paniceum*, and other pests of furniture, books, and stored food are related to the death-watch beetle.

English author Francis Grose, in his 1790 book, *A Provincial Glossary; with a Collection of Local Proverbs, and Popular Superstitions*, included the beetle in his list of "Omens Portending Death." The list begins with such omens as the howling of a dog, a lump of coal in the shape of a coffin, and a child who does not cry when sprinkled in baptismal water. The beetle was another sign that the end was near. He wrote, "The ticking of a death-watch is an omen of the death of someone in the house wherein it is heard."

The beetle was another sign that the end was near.

But the beetle's morbid song is hardly its worst quality. These dull, gray-brown beetles bore through moist wood, creating tiny entry and exit holes packed with the powdery residue they leave behind. They prefer hardwood timbers that have already been colonized by fungus, which explains why magnificent old oak buildings in England hold so much appeal. Death-watch beetles can also be found in books and heavy antique furniture. Under the most advantageous circumstances, they may live for five to seven years, undermining homes, cathedrals, and libraries.

The larvae in particular love to live in and consume old, damp buildings. In fact, Oxford's famous Bodleian Library recently required a new roof to save its decorated ceiling from the destruction these creatures had caused. Many homeowners have found their rafters turned to powder after decades of quiet chewing by this destructive pest.

An entomologist writing for *Harper's Magazine* in 1861 said it best when she described a trip to visit a friend in the country:

> The first night I fancied I should have gone mad before morning. The walls of the bed-room were papered, and from them beat, as it were, a thousand watches—tick, tick, tick . . . But at last the welcome morning dawned, and early I was down in the library; even here every book, on shelf above shelf, was riotous with tick, tick, tick . . . The house was a huge clock, with thousands of pendulums ticking from morning till night. I was careful not to allow my great discomfort to annoy others. I argued, what they could tolerate, surely I could; and in a few days habit had rendered the fearful, dreaded ticking a positive necessity.

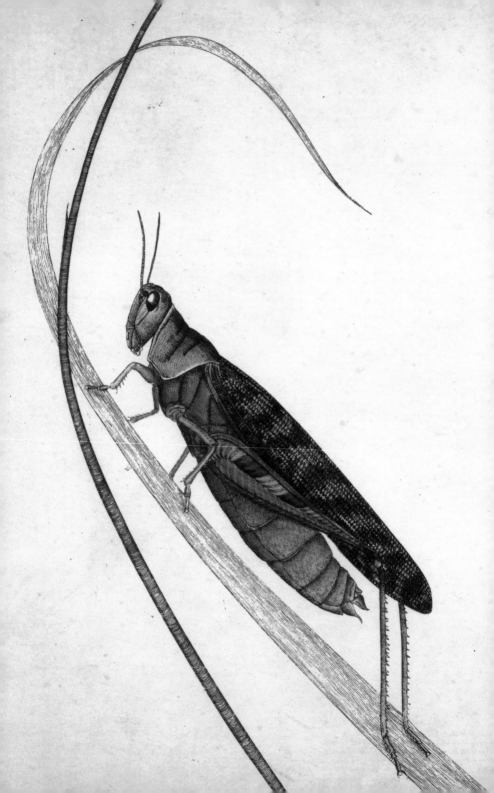

ROCKY MOUNTAIN LOCUST
Melanoplus spretus

A plague of locusts swept across the American West in the summer of 1875. Farmers watched in horror as a dark shape rose from the horizon and advanced across the sky, moving faster than any thunderstorm or tornado. The sun dimmed and vanished, the sky filled with a strange buzzing, crackling sound, and then, all at once, the locusts descended.

SIZE: 1 3/8 in (3.5 cm)

FAMILY: Acrididae

HABITAT: Meadows and prairies in the American West

DISTRIBUTION: North America

MEET THE RELATIVES: Not all grasshoppers are capable of turning into locusts. Of the 11,000 species of grasshoppers, only a dozen or so are known for becoming locusts under stress.

It happened so quickly that parents had to grab their children and run for shelter. Locusts swarmed over every inch of the cornfields, covered homes and barns, devoured trees and bushes, and even massed indoors. There seemed to be no end to the assault. Millions dropped out of the sky, but millions more moved on to the next county and the one after that.

The sheer volume of locusts that a swarm delivers is almost impossible to grasp. Witnesses reported tree branches breaking under the weight of the insects. A layer of insects six inches deep covered the ground. The locusts clogged rivers, and their bodies washed into the Great Salt Lake by the ton, creating a putrid wall of brined corpses that reached six feet tall and extended for two miles.

The size of that ferocious swarm was estimated at 198,000 square miles—larger than the state of California—and it contained about 3.5 trillion locusts. They completely destroyed crops and bred with frightening speed and efficiency—one square inch of soil could hold 150 eggs. A typical farm could be left with no crops and enough eggs buried in the soil to produce thirty million more locusts. When the larvae hatched in the spring, it looked like the ground was boiling with them.

This pestilence created widespread poverty and starvation across the Great Plains of the United States. Some states offered locust bounties to farmers, paying a few dollars for a bushel of eggs or nymphs in an attempt to rid the land of the insects while providing income for its destitute citizens. Some enterprising farmers turned their flocks of chickens and turkeys loose on the swarms, hoping that the free protein source would turn a tragedy into an opportunity. But instead, the birds gorged themselves on the bugs, literally eating themselves to death. The diet of locusts even tainted their flesh, making the birds inedible. Farmers set fires in their fields, doused the soil with kerosene, and resorted to any poison or potion they could get their hands on, but nothing worked. The locusts continued to sweep across the landscape throughout the late 1800s, leaving devastation and mass starvation in their wake.

Parents had to grab their children and run for shelter.

Little was understood at the time about the life cycle of the Rocky Mountain locust. Entomologists now know that a locust is little more than a grasshopper under pressure. A Russian entomologist named Boris Uvarov, working in the 1920s, proved that certain species of ordinary-looking grasshoppers were capable of undergoing a remarkable transformation during times of stress.

Grasshoppers usually forage alone, spreading out across large areas when food is plentiful. But during a drought, the creatures may be crowded together, and that proximity brings on chemical changes that cause the females to lay eggs that are very different from the ones they typically produce. The nymphs that hatch from those eggs grow longer wings, have a propensity to live more closely together and travel in dense packs, and are themselves capable of laying eggs that can survive longer periods of dormancy. The nymphs even change color. In essence, a fairly benign, stable grasshopper population transforms itself into a migratory plague of locusts capable of swarming and devouring everything in its path.

This explains why the settlers claimed to have never seen these particular locusts before the ominous swarms arrived, and why plagues of locusts have often been regarded as having some divine origin. They are entirely unfamiliar creatures, having transformed themselves from ordinary grasshoppers to larger, darker, never-before-seen invaders.

Even more mysterious, though, was their sudden disappearance. The swarms diminished in size through the turn of the century, and eventually vanished altogether. The Rocky Mountain locust—the grasshopper known as *Melanoplus spretus*—has not been seen alive since 1902. Although other species of grasshoppers swarmed across the West during the Great Depression, they were not nearly as destructive, nor as widespread.

Ironically, scientists now believe that farmers managed to eradicate the locust by doing what they do best—farming. As they turned prairie land into cornfields and cow pastures, they destroyed the insects' only permanent breeding grounds, a series of rich river valleys along the Rocky Mountains where the entire population returned every year to breed. *Melanoplus spretus* now appears to be extinct—much to the relief of American farmers.

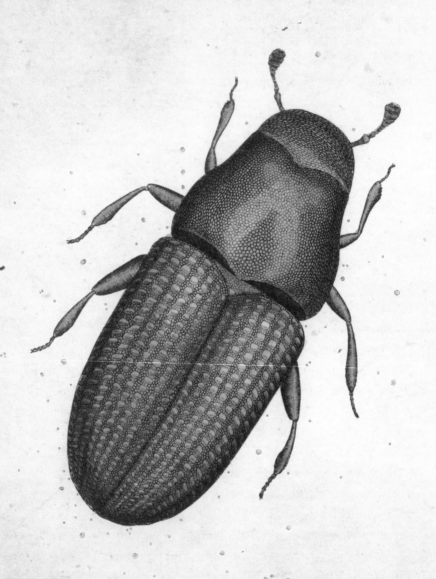

MOUNTAIN PINE BEETLE
Dendroctonus ponderosae

By the 1930s, a full-scale war was underway in the American West. A bug was devouring the forests. The United States spent millions of dollars studying it, but the efforts of the government were no match for the mountain pine beetle. By the 1980s, the *New York Times* reported that the insect was ravaging America's forests, taking out 3.4 million acres in the American West. And 2009 was even worse, with 6.5 million acres destroyed in the United States, and an astonishing thirty-five million acres lost in British Columbia—an area roughly the size of New York State.

SIZE: 1/8– 5/16 in (3–8 mm)

FAMILY: Curculionidae

HABITAT: Pine forests

DISTRIBUTION: Throughout North America, from New Mexico, Colorado, Wyoming, and Montana to the West Coast; in Canada, throughout British Columbia and parts of Alberta

MEET THE RELATIVES: Related to a wide range of other destructive bark beetles and weevils, including the southern pine beetle (*D. frontalis*), found throughout Central America and the southern United States, and the European spruce bark beetle *Ips typographus*, which has devastated spruce forests in central Europe and Scandinavia.

The mountain pine beetle—a minuscule creature that doesn't get any bigger than a grain of rice—burrows into the bark of a pine tree until it reaches living tissue. There, she eats and lays her eggs, sending out a pheromone, a chemical used to attract other beetles, to

Diseased trees turn red as they die, making a vibrant green pine forest look more like the leafy New England woods in fall.

let them know that she's found a good tree. The tree tries to fight back, excreting a sticky resin that can kill the beetles. Usually, that defense isn't enough, and a mass attack gets underway. As the insects burrow into the tree, they transmit a disease called blue stain fungus that essentially clogs the tree's tissue, making it impossible to transport water up to the leaf canopy.

The larvae tunnel away from their egg gallery and spend the winter underneath the bark. They keep themselves warm by turning carbohydrates into glycerol, which acts as a kind of antifreeze to keep them from freezing to death. In the spring, the glycerol is converted back to carbohydrates and serves as an energy source while the larvae become pupae under the bark. They emerge as adults in July, mate briefly, and complete the cycle. Mountain pine beetles live for a year, spending all but a few days of that time under the bark of a tree.

In a typical forest, the beetles will start by attacking old, weak, or diseased trees. By going after the older trees first, they actually help "recycle" aged trees and make room for the next generation. But many foresters agree that decades of fire suppression have led to forests with dense populations of older trees, rather than a diverse mix of generations. Now all these older trees are under attack at once. A long, deep freeze may kill off the larvae under the bark, but recent warmer winters have made it easy for large populations to survive and reproduce.

The devastation brought on by the mountain pine beetle is easy to see from the air. Diseased trees turn red as they die, making a vibrant green pine forest look more like the leafy New England woods in fall. Unfortunately, there is no good way to control the beetle. Natural predators like woodpeckers eat mountain pine beetles, but they can't stop an outbreak. Chemical controls cost too much to make sense, and time-consuming treatments like peeling the bark away to expose (and kill) the larvae are not practical on a large scale.

Foresters focus instead on prevention, which includes thinning trees. In addition, they allow some natural fires to burn forested land, which encourages new growth. Now the only question is what to do with the diseased trees. Some experts suggest turning them into wood chips that can be used to make ethanol fuel, or pressing them into pellets to fuel stoves. In Vancouver, British Columbia, where the beetle has hit hardest, the 2010 Winter Olympics arena featured a roof made from over a million board feet of wood infested by the pine beetle.

FORMOSAN SUBTERRANEAN TERMITE
Coptotermes formosanus

SIZE: 1/2 in (1.5 cm)

FAMILY: Rhinotermitidae

HABITAT: Found underground, in trees, or in attics and crawl spaces of wood structures

DISTRIBUTION: Taiwan, China, Japan, Hawaii, South Africa, Sri Lanka, and the southeastern United States

MEET THE RELATIVES: About 2800 species of termites have been identified worldwide.

"Judging from recent news stories," said entomologist Mark Hunter in 2000, "the Formosan termite appears determined to consume the historic French Quarter of New Orleans. These termites destroy creosote-treated utility poles and wharves, the switch boxes of underground traffic lights, underground telephone cables, live trees and shrubs and the seals on high pressure water lines." At that time, he predicted that this invasive Asian termite would be the greatest challenge in the war between humans and insects in the twenty-first century.

Unfortunately, Hurricane Katrina proved him right. One of the most devastating natural disaster in United States history killed more than 1800 people and displaced three-quarters of a million, making it the largest mass migration since the Dust Bowl of the 1930s. When Hurricane Katrina damages were finally tallied, they reached almost $100 billion. And as New Orleans started to rebuild, it became clear that the pest that has plagued this city for decades may have played a role in its destruction when Katrina hit in 2005. The seams of the floodwalls that were supposed to protect the city were made of sugarcane waste, a treat that Formosan termites cannot resist.

Could any of this have been prevented? Seventeen years before Katrina, the Formosan termite lost its most dedicated foe. Jeffery LaFage, a Louisiana State University AgCenter entomologist, was out for dinner in the French Quarter in 1989 to celebrate the start of his new program to eliminate termites from the Quarter. As he walked through the Quarter with a friend after dinner,

The seams of the floodwalls that were supposed to protect the city were made of sugarcane waste, a treat that Formosan termites cannot resist.

a robber shot and killed Jeffrey. His death set termite control in the area back by years.

Fellow AgCenter entomologist Gregg Henderson took up the fight. He sounded the alarm about the infestation of termites in the floodwalls five years before Katrina came ashore, then watched in horror as his worst predictions came true. "I remember watching the news as the floodwalls and levees broke," he said. "I started to get that sick feeling, when you know something's wrong." While poor planning and maintenance certainly contributed to their failure, the role of the Formosan termite could not be overlooked. Henderson has since developed a program to lure termites away from the floodwalls, to places where they could be more easily captured and killed, but he's been unable to get officials interested in his ideas.

Formosan termites have been a problem in New Orleans for decades. The creatures seem to have arrived aboard ships returning to port after World War II. The damp, tropical climate and abundant supply of old wood frame buildings in New Orleans offer the perfect breeding ground for the pest. The French Quarter's row houses make it especially easy for termites to flourish. Any efforts at control undertaken in one building would simply encourage the insects to move next door. Before Katrina hit, the city's residents were losing an estimated $300 million per year to termite damage.

A Formosan termite queen can live for up to twenty-five years, enjoying a steady supply of food delivered by her workers. In addition, the king termite's sole job is to mate with her. Every day she lays hundreds—or perhaps thousands—of eggs. When the larvae hatch, they are fed by worker termites, and then grow up to be either workers themselves, which eat wood and feed the colony; soldiers, which use specialized defenses to kill attackers; or nymphs that develop into supplemental kings and queens or alates, winged creatures that are capable of becoming kings and queens; of their own colonies. The swarms of alates around lampposts in the French Quarter from late April through June are so dense that they actually dim the lights and send tourists running.

Some pest control experts hoped that Hurricane Katrina would have one silver lining—a mass drowning of Formosan termites. Unfortunately, the termites were not stopped. The insects build homes for themselves out of digested wood, feces, and spit. These cartons contain intricate networks of tiny chambers and corridors that hold colonies of several million. The cartons kept most colonies safe and dry throughout the hurricane and the flooding that followed. When home and business owners abandoned their buildings, no one remained to continue the careful regimen of pest control they'd been following to limit the termites. The conditions were perfect for the termite to rise again.

CORPSE EATERS

The science of forensic entomology—the study of insects to determine the time, location, or circumstances of a death—is not particularly new. A book called *The Washing Away of Wrongs*, written in China in 1235, described how an infestation of flies on a corpse could provide clues in a crime investigation. It even told of a murder that was solved by watching what flies did when the villagers came together and laid out their sickles, sharp farming tools, for inspection. The flies landed on one sickle in particular, perhaps because traces of tissue and blood were present. Confronted with this evidence, the owner of the sickle confessed to having used it to commit the crime.

> By examining the species of insects that inhabit a corpse, and looking at the information in relation to weather data and other information about the crime scene, it is possible to estimate how long the person has been wounded and whether the corpse was moved at any point during the crime.

These methods are still in use today. In 2003, University of California, Davis, entomologist Lynn Kimsey received a visit from a police officer and two FBI agents. They wanted to know if she could inspect the bugs smashed against a car's radiator and air filter to determine what states the car had driven through. Their theory was that the suspect, a man named Vincent Brothers, had driven from Ohio to California to murder his family. He claimed he never left Ohio. Kimsey agreed to have a look.

There were thirty different insects on the car, but they weren't intact: she had to make her identifications from fragments of wings and legs and smashed bodies. She found a grasshopper, a wasp, and two other bugs that could have been picked up only during a drive through the West. At the 2007 trial, she testified for five hours, and the jury eventually convicted Brothers of murder.

The most common use of forensic entomology is in establishing the time frame within which a death occurred. By examining the species of insects that inhabit a corpse, and looking at the information in relation to weather data and other information about the crime scene, it is possible to estimate how long the person has been wounded and whether the corpse was moved at any point during the crime.

Blow flies, also called carrion flies, come from the family Calliphoridae. These blue-green flies are usually the first on the scene after a death, thanks in part to their ability to smell a corpse from over a hundred feet (thirty meters) away. They have been known to arrive as quickly as ten minutes after a death occurs, and may lay thousands of eggs in the body. The extent to which those eggs have hatched and moved through their stages of development can help pinpoint the time of a recent death. The answers don't always come quickly, though. Sometimes, entomologists have to collect the eggs and wait for them to hatch, then count backward to determine the estimated time of death.

Blow flies in the *Calliphora* genus develop quickly from egg to larva to pupa, and that process is accelerated in hot weather. So it is important for investigators to know what the temperature has been so that they can correlate that information with the size of the creature.

Burying beetles, members of the genus *Nicrophorus*, are attracted to carcasses by their scent and usually turn up to find out if the body is something they are capable of burying. Their reasons have to do with their unique life cycle. When burying beetles find a dead mouse, bird, or other small animal, they actually dig a hole and line it with fur or feathers they strip from the body, creating a kind of crypt. Often, several pairs of beetles will join together in this effort, spending an entire day on the burial process. Once the corpse is completely covered—and therefore protected from other predators—the females lay their eggs inside the crypt so their young will have a food source when they hatch. They even stick around to tend to the brood, making them one of the few insects that actually care for their young.

In the case of a human carcass, the beetles are often found under the body, burying small bits of flesh and possibly tampering with important evidence. They may also lay eggs inside the body since it is too large to bury. There have been cases of the beetles breeding inside stab wounds, for instance. They eat blow fly larvae and sometimes carry tiny mites that feed on blow fly eggs as well, so their arrival on the scene can interfere with the critical information that blow fly eggs and larvae provide.

Mites arrive in stages as well. The first to arrive are gamasid mites, which ride around on beetles and feed on the eggs of the first wave of flies. Later in the process, tyroglyphid mites, also known as mold mites, show up to feed on mold, fungi, and dry skin.

Rove beetles in the family Staphylinidae may be among the next insects to appear as the deceased enters a not-quite-as-fresh stage. They are attracted primarily to the fly larvae, which means that they tend to show up and devour whatever evidence the first wave of flies have left behind.

Skin beetles in the family Dermestidae are called late-stage scavengers because they often appear a couple of months after death has occurred. These are the beetles used in history museums to clean animal skeletons being prepared for display. Another family of beetles may turn up later in a corpse's decomposition—the so-called ham beetles in the family Cleridae, which get their name from their habit of infesting dried meats. They have been found in tombs and on Egyptian mummies.

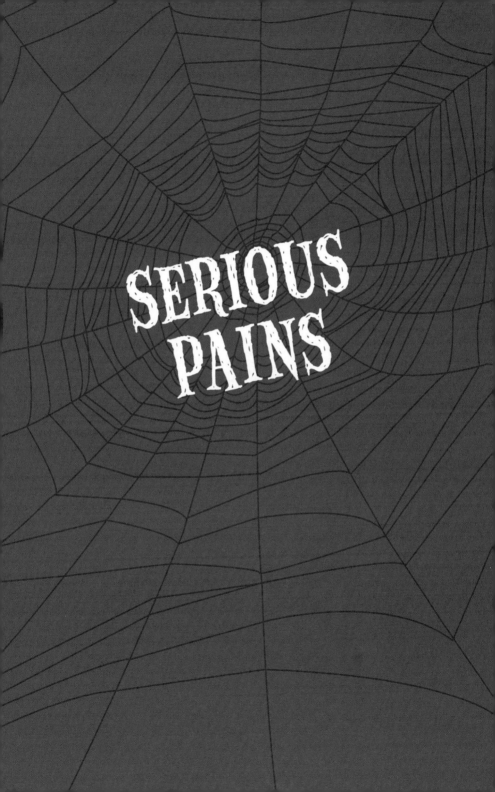

ASIAN GIANT HORNET
Vespa mandarinia japonica

In the past few years, during dry summers, public health officials in Tokyo have warned citizens that the world's largest hornet, with the most painful sting, may be in their midst. The so-called Asian giant hornet, known locally as the yak-killer hornet, delivers a venomous sting that contains high levels of the pain-inducing compounds normally found in bee or wasp stings. It also contains a deadly neurotoxin called mandaratoxin that can be fatal. The world's leading expert on the giant hornet, Dr. Masato Ono, describes the sting as feeling like "a hot nail through my leg." Worst of all, the sting attracts other hornets to the victim through the pheromones it leaves behind, increasing the likelihood that a person will be stung several times.

In Japan, these hornets are called *suzumebachi*, which translates to "sparrow wasp." Measuring two inches (five centimeters) from head to tail, they are so large that when they fly they actually

SIZE: 2 in (5 cm)

FAMILY: Vespidae

HABITAT: Forests and, increasingly, cities

DISTRIBUTION: Japan, China, Taiwan, Korea, and other areas throughout Asia

MEET THE RELATIVES: Giant Asian hornets are related to other hornets, which are distinguished from wasps by their larger heads and more rounded abdomens. The European hornet, *Vespa crabro*, delivers a nasty sting when disturbed, but it is no deadlier than the sting of any other hornet.

The world's leading expert on the giant hornet, Dr. Masato Ono, describes the sting as feeling like "a hot nail through my leg."

resemble small birds. During hot summers, they can be seen in Japanese cities, foraging in garbage cans for bits of discarded fish to carry back to their young. Because they are so willing to venture into urban areas in search of food, about forty people die every year after being stung by the massive hornets.

If such a creature is frightening to humans, imagine what it must look like to a honeybee. Scientists observing wild colonies of the Japanese honeybee *Apis cerana japonica* have long known that the colonies are vulnerable to attacks from the giant hornets. Usually, a single hornet shows up first to scout the area. It kills a few bees and brings them back to the hive to feed its young. After a few of these trips, the hornet tags the hive by smearing it with pheromones. The pheromones signal to the other hornets that it is time for an attack.

A gang of about thirty hornets descend on the hive. Within a few hours, these monstrous creatures massacre as many as thirty thousand of the small honeybees, ripping off their heads and tossing their bodies on the ground. Once they've killed the bees, the hornets occupy the empty hive for about ten days, robbing it of its honey and stealing the bee larvae to feed their own children.

Recently, Dr. Ono and his colleagues at Tamagawa University discovered that the Japanese honeybees had devised an extraordinarily clever way of attacking back. The first time a solitary hornet approaches the hive, worker bees retreat inside, luring the hornet to the entrance. Then an army of over five hundred honeybees swarm the hornet, beating their wings furiously and raising the surrounding temperature to 116 degrees—just hot enough to kill the hornet.

This is a dangerous procedure for the honeybees. If the swarm becomes just a few degrees hotter, they will die as well. In fact, some worker bees do die in the struggle, but the swarm pushes them out of the way and carries on until the hornet is dead. It can take twenty minutes for the honeybees to bake their enemy to death. While it is not unusual for insects to mount a group defense against an enemy, this is the only known case of using body heat alone to defeat an attacker.

The hornets' extraordinary strength led Japanese researchers to test an extract of their stomach juices as a performance enhancement for athletes. They discovered that adult hornets, which can fly incredible distances in search of food, are actually unable to eat much solid food themselves because their digestive tracts are so small. They do, however, bring dead insects back to their young to eat. After the larvae have finished their meal, the adults tap on their heads, which prompts the larvae to offer up a "kiss" consisting of a few drops of clear liquid. The adults drink this liquid, using it as a source of fuel. The Japanese scientists harvested the clear liquid, one drop at a time, from larvae they found in over eighty hornets' nests. In the laboratory, they demonstrated that both mice and university graduate students showed reduced fatigue and an increased ability to turn fat into energy after drinking the juice.

Marathon runner Naoko Takahashi, who won an Olympic gold medal in Sydney in 2000, credited her success to this "hornet juice." As a natural substance, it didn't violate the International Olympic Committee rules on performance enhancers. Today, an athletic drink called hornet juice is marketed to athletes with the claim that it boosts endurance. However, these drinks don't contain actual extracts from giant hornet larva, just a mix of amino acids intended to mimic the powerful juice.

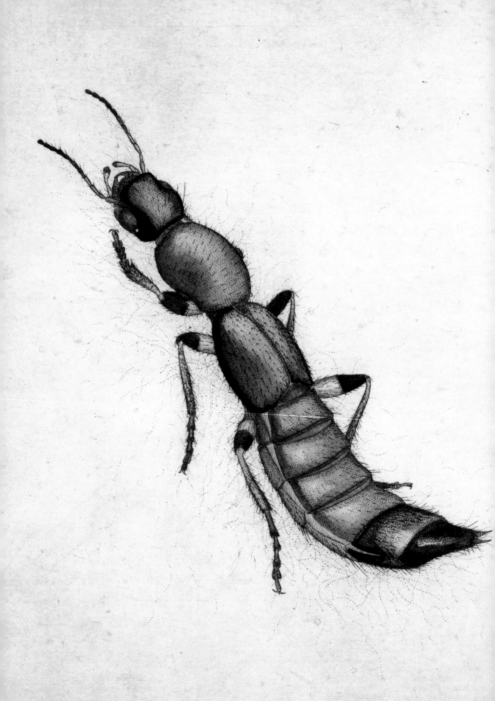

PAEDERUS BEETLE
Paederus sp.

Heavy El Niño rains brought more than floods to Nairobi in 1998. The wet weather created an explosion of Paederus beetles, also called Nairobi flies for their long association with the region. The beetles creep into schools and homes, attracted to the lights. They don't bite and they don't sting, so their presence would be only a minor irritant if not for one fact: when the lights go out, the bugs tend to let go of the lamps and land on whoever may be sitting, or sleeping, below them. The natural tendency is to swat at the bug when it lands, but crushing this beetle releases a surprisingly potent poison called pederin.

Nothing much happens when the poison first hits the skin. But the next day, a rash develops, and a few days after that, blisters appear. It takes a couple of weeks for the raw, exposed skin to begin

SIZE: 1/4 in (6–7 mm)

FAMILY: Staphylinidae

HABITAT: Damp environments, including woods, meadows, and aquatic areas

DISTRIBUTION: Almost worldwide, particularly in India, Southeast Asia, China, Japan, the Middle East, Europe, Africa, and Australia

MEET THE RELATIVES: There are roughly 620 species of Paederus beetles worldwide. They are a member of the rove beetle family, which includes many interesting beetles, such as the devil's coach-horse beetle *Ocypus olens*, a large European beetle that looks threatening and will bite if provoked but is otherwise harmless.

to heal, and during that time, people may develop infections if they don't keep the wounds clean. A single beetle can raise a welt the size of a quarter on the skin. A drop of its poison, rubbed into the eye, brings on excruciating pain and temporary blindness, a condition called Nairobi eye. The problem in Kenya grew so severe that the Ministry of Health issued warnings urging citizens to keep lights turned off at night, sleep under mosquito nets, and get in the habit of blowing the insects off their skin rather than swatting them. Health officials label this strategy as "brush, don't crush."

In Iraq, the bugs swarm around the very lights where troops may be stationed in the evening.

Outbreaks of Paederus dermatitis have been a vexing problem on military bases around the world, where bright lights attract the bugs and soldiers may not know to avoid them. In Iraq, the bugs swarm around the very lights where troops may be stationed in the evening. And while bug zappers are widely used on military bases, making the area immediately around them a safe place for soldiers to congregate, the Paederus beetles are drawn to the light but are not killed by the zappers. Soldiers are urged to keep their sleeves rolled down and their uniforms tucked in, difficult tasks in the desert heat.

The Paederus beetle is a small, skinny creature with alternating red and black segments and extremely short wing covers that don't resemble wings at all (some species are not even capable of flight). The beetle could easily be mistaken for a large ant. The beetles do prey on smaller bugs, including some serious agricultural pests, so farmers generally welcome them despite the risks they pose to workers in the field.

There is some speculation that the Paederus beetle is the source of a mysterious legend about a bird that excreted poison droppings. Ctesias, a Greek physician who wrote an account of India in the fifth century BCE, described a poison that appeared in the droppings of a tiny orange bird. "Its dung has a peculiar property," he wrote, "for if a quantity of it no bigger than a grain of millet be dissolved into a potion, it would be enough to kill a man by the fall of evening." No trace of this poisonous bird, which he called the dikairon, has ever been found. Some historians speculate that the actual poison was not a bird dropping but the bright orange and black Paederus beetle, which sometimes lives in the nests of birds and could be mistaken for droppings. A beetle fitting this description was also known in Chinese medicine as far back as 739 CE as a poison so strong it could remove tattoos, boils, or ringworms. The Paederus beetle may have medical use today as well—its poison, pederin, inhibits cell growth and is under investigation as a possible antitumor agent for use in cancer treatment.

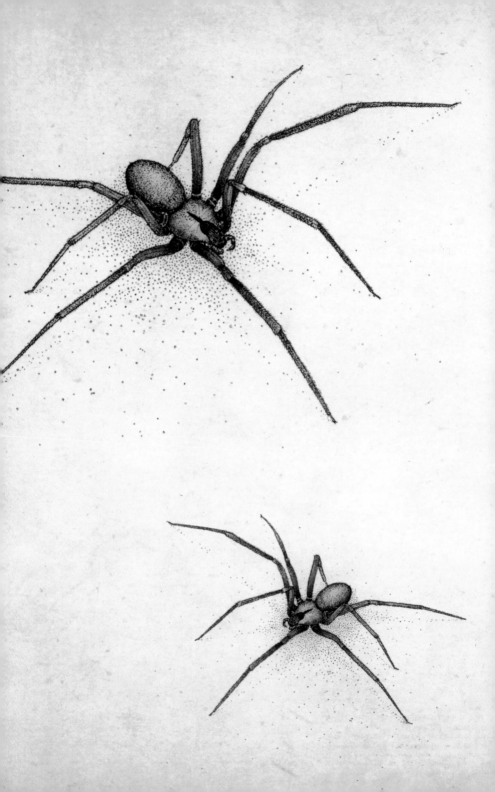

BROWN RECLUSE
Loxosceles reclusa

SIZE: Up to ³⁄₈ in (9.5 mm)

FAMILY: Sicariidae

HABITAT: Dry, sheltered, undisturbed places like woodpiles, sheds, and undergrowth

DISTRIBUTION: Central and southern United States

MEET THE RELATIVES: Recluse spiders are related to another genus of six-eyed spiders called the six-eyed sand spider.

Arachnologists, or scientists who study spiders and other arachnids, insist that there are only two ways to accurately diagnose a brown recluse bite: to capture the spider in the act and get it identified, or to have a dermatologist biopsy a fresh bite wound. Without that evidence, it is entirely likely that the painful, rotting lesion that sends a person running to the doctor was caused by something other than this dreaded spider—and the misdiagnosis is often more deadly than the spider bite itself.

That's not to say that the brown recluse doesn't bite, or that its bite isn't painful. A severe brown recluse bite is a nasty, swollen skin sore with dead cells in the center. These bites form a red, white, and blue bull's-eye pattern. The center is a bluish-gray spot that represents dying flesh. Around that is a white circle where blood flow is restricted. And a painful red area creates the outside edge. Contrary to rumors, most people recover from these wounds quickly, with only the more severe cases lasting a month or two. Permanent scars are possible, but uncommon.

There have been news reports of deaths caused by brown recluse bites, but these accounts are disputed by some of the nation's leading brown recluse experts. What accounts for the number of misdiagnosed brown recluse bites? The spider itself was virtually unknown until the second half of the twentieth century, when a handful of news accounts placed the blame for mysterious wounds with this little-known spider. Now it seems that every person with an unexplained sore is able to find a small brown spider nearby. The brown recluse is easily confused with other species. There are many arachnids that resemble it, and several that even have the same violin-shaped marking on the back. The only way to accurately identify a brown recluse is to look deep into its eyes—they have six of them, arranged in three pairs. Experts also look for a uniformly brown abdomen covered in fine hairs; brown, smooth legs; and small size. The body of a brown recluse is never more than 9.5 mm in length.

A family in Kansas collected over two thousand brown recluse spiders in and around their home in just six months.

These spiders are found in central and southern areas of the United States, but reports of their bites persist nationwide. To date, the brown recluse has been positively identified in only sixteen states: Texas, Oklahoma, Kansas, Missouri, Arkansas, Louisiana, Mississippi, Alabama, Tennessee, Kentucky, and parts of neighboring states, including Nebraska, Iowa, Illinois, Indiana, Ohio, and Georgia.

Reports of the spider in other parts of the country are so persistent that frustrated arachnologists have offered rewards to anyone who can send them an actual brown recluse from an area where they are not known to live. One California scientist called it the "Show Me the Spider" challenge. After years of attempting to locate a brown recluse in the state, University of California entomologists have declared that the brown recluse definitively does not live in California, and even sightings of the state's native desert recluse spider are rare.

But for people who do live in places where the spider is found, it can be disturbing to realize how many of them live nearby. A family in Kansas collected over two thousand brown recluse spiders in and around their home in just six months. Remarkably, no one was bitten in the six years the family lived in the house. A recluse usually won't bite unless it is quite literally forced against the skin. For this reason, the best advice experts can offer is to shake out camping gear, as well as bedding or clothing that's been in storage or crumpled on the floor for a long time. Avoid the recluse, and the recluse will avoid you.

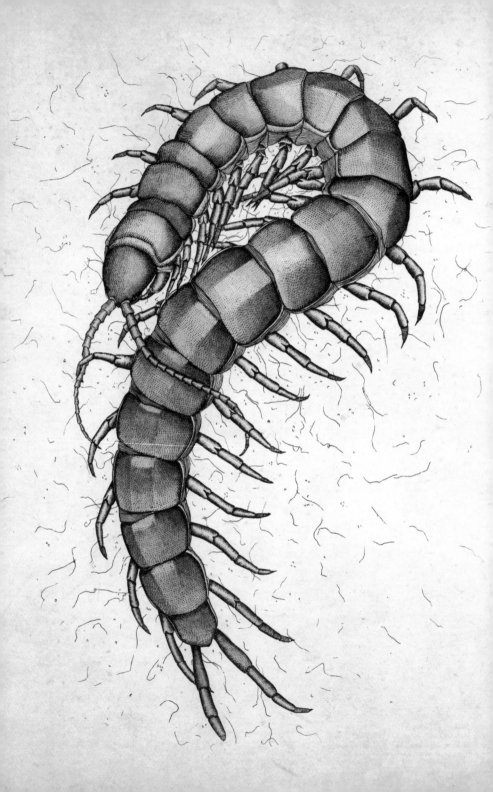

GIANT CENTIPEDE
Scolopendra gigantean

I n 2005, a thirty-two year-old man was watching television in his London home when he heard a strange rustling sound under a stack of papers. He got up, expecting to find a mouse. Instead a nine-inch-long, prehistoric-looking creature with more legs than he could count scuttled away. Fortunately, he had the presence of mind to grab a plastic container and scoop it inside without touching it.

SIZE: Up to 12 in (30 cm)

FAMILY: Scolopendridae

HABITAT: Moist environments such as the undersides of rocks, leaf litter, and the forest floor

DISTRIBUTION: South American forests

MEET THE RELATIVES: There are about 2500 species of centipedes around the world. The other members of the giant centipede's family are found mostly in the tropics.

The next morning, he took it to London's Natural History Museum, where an entomologist peered into the bag, expecting to find the sort of run-of-the-mill insect that visitors bring to the museum every day. But when he "produced this beast from his bag I was staggered," the entomologist told reporters. "Not even I expected to be presented with this."

The "beast" in question was the world's largest centipede, *Scolopendra gigantea*. This enormous South American creature can reach a foot (thirty centimeters) long, and its bite delivers a powerful dose of venom. It may have twenty-one or twenty-three segments.

From each segment protrudes one pair of legs. The legs on the first segment are a pair of venom-bearing claws called forcipules. The bite of the giant centipede is powerful enough to cause swelling, pain that radiates up and down the limb where the bite occurred, and even a small amount of necrosis, or dead flesh. Nausea, dizziness, and other such symptoms are common with a bite as severe as this, but the wounds usually require only simple medical care.

The centipedes were hanging from the cave by their last few legs and catching bats in midair as they flew by, demonstrating a rather frightening level of forethought and ingenuity.

Although people will most likely survive the bite of a giant centipede, small creatures like lizards, frogs, birds, and rats are not so lucky. A team of researchers in Venezuela found one of these giant centipedes hanging upside down from a cave wall, happily munching away on a small bat. After observing the same behavior several times, the researchers realized that the centipedes were hanging from the cave by their last few legs and catching bats in midair as they flew by, demonstrating a rather frightening level of forethought and ingenuity.

Despite their name, centipedes don't all have a hundred legs. They are distinguished from millipedes in that they have one, not two, pair of legs attached to each segment. The precise number of legs varies by species. And although all centipedes do bite, many are too diminutive to inflict much pain, and some have such small, soft mouthparts that they can't even pierce human skin. (Still, never touch a centipede with bare hands.) Found in homes throughout North America, the house centipede *Scutigera coleoptrata* may look intimidating, with its fifteen pairs of strangely long legs, but its bite delivers little or no pain. It eats bed bugs, silverfish, carpet beetles, and cockroaches, so its presence could signal that a house has one of those infestations!

Centipedes lack the kind of waxy covering that keeps some insects from drying out, so they must stay in moist areas to survive. They breathe through tiny openings behind their legs, and the amount of water they exhale through these openings puts them at even greater risk of dehydration.

The female giant centipede will brood over her eggs until they hatch, even protecting them from predators the way a bird in a nest guards her young.

The pain inflicted by a centipede is mostly related to its size and the amount of venom it injects—the bigger the centipede, the more venom. People living in the southwestern United States have good reason to fear the giant redheaded centipede *Scolopendra heros*, which at about eight inches (twenty centimeters) long, can deliver a whopping bite. A military physician who has been bitten repeatedly by this species described the pain as a "ten" on a scale of one to ten, and reported that over-the-counter medication offered no relief, but that the discomfort and swelling receded completely after a day or two.

And as for the British man who found the enormous centipede in his living room? Eventually, the man's neighbor came forward and confessed that he had purchased the centipede at a local pet store and intended to keep it as a pet. (The giants can live for up to ten years, making this a long-term commitment.) The creature was returned to its owner who, ideally, would keep a closer eye on it.

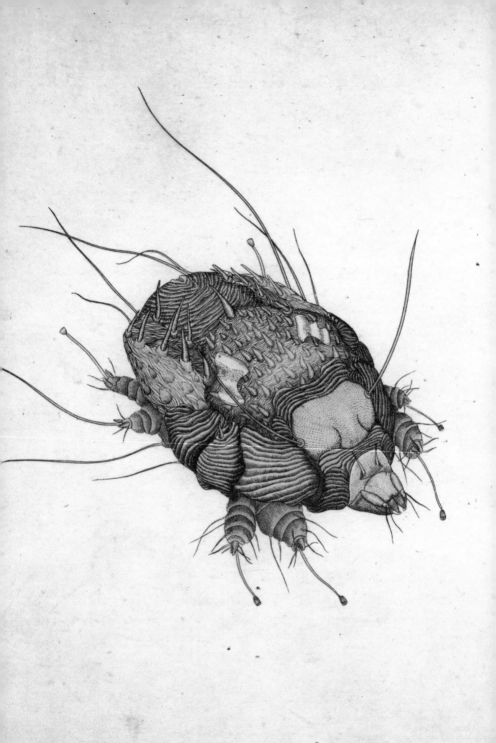

SCABIES MITE
Sarcoptes scabiei var. hominis

SIZE: Up to 0.45 mm

FAMILY: Sarcoptidae

HABITAT: On or very near its host

DISTRIBUTION: Worldwide

MEET THE RELATIVES: A variety of scabies mites infest humans, wild animals, and domesticated animals. The mite *S. scabiei canis* causes a type of mange in dogs known as sarcoptic mange.

Dr. Francesco Carlo Antommarchi had the good fortune—or misfortune—to serve as one of Napoleon Bonaparte's last physicians during his exile to Saint Helena, an island in the South Atlantic Ocean. Difficult and demanding, Bonaparte had suffered from a number of ailments over the years, including digestive problems, liver disease, and a mysterious rash. On October 31, 1819, just a year and a half before Napoleon's death, the doctor recorded this bizarre exchange:

The Emperor was uneasy and agitated: I advised him to take some calming medicine which I pointed out to him. "Thanks, Doctor," said he; "I have something better than your pharmacy. The moment approaches, I feel, when Nature will relieve herself." In saying this he threw himself upon a chair, and seizing his left thigh, tore it open with a kind of eager delight. His scars opened anew, and the blood gushed out. "I told you so, Doctor; I am now better. I have my periods of crisis, and when they occur I am saved."

Antommarchi was not the first to observe Napoleon tearing apart his own skin to relieve some terrible pain. One of his servants wrote that "on several occasions I saw him dig his nails into his thigh so vehemently that the blood came." He was sometimes so covered in blood during military campaigns that his soldiers thought he had been wounded, when in fact he was just scratching himself. We may never know exactly what drove Napoleon into such a frenzy, but at least one doctor who treated him diagnosed the rash as scabies.

Although it was not well understood at the time, the scabies mite afflicted troops during the Napoleonic wars and virtually all wars since. Crowded conditions, the necessity of wearing the same clothing day after day without washing, and mass migrations of poor people during wartime all contribute to the spread of scabies. There were some attempts made during the late 1600s to persuade the medical community that scabies was caused by a parasite, but those ideas were largely ignored. Napoleon's doctors would have most likely believed that scabies was caused by an "imbalance of the humours," the fluids in the body.

By 1865, decades after Napoleon's death, it was finally understood that scabies was caused by the actions of a nearly invisible mite. An adult female burrows into the skin, usually around the hands and wrists, and lays a few eggs every day. The eggs hatch and the larvae move into an upper layer of the skin, where they form tiny dwellings called molting pouches. They molt into nymphs and then into adult mites, which will mate just once during their short lives, all the while occupying this space under the skin. Once pregnant, the females leave their burrows at last, and walk along their host's body until they find another suitable location to start a new family. In all, a scabies mite lives for one to two months, spending almost all that time under the skin of its host.

People who are infested with scabies mites may not experience any symptoms at all for the first month or two of the infestation. Over time, however, they develop a severe reaction to the mites themselves, not to mention the waste products left under the skin. Sometimes, a rash spreads all over the abdomen, shoulders, and backside, even when no mites can be found. Because the mite can live a few days away from its host, it is theoretically possible to transmit scabies through clothing, bedsheets, and toys, although the most common means of transmission is skin-to-skin contact. While Napoleon suffered his whole life from a probable scabies infection, doctors today can treat the condition with a topical cream.

The scabies mite afflicted troops during the Napoleonic wars and virtually all wars since.

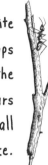

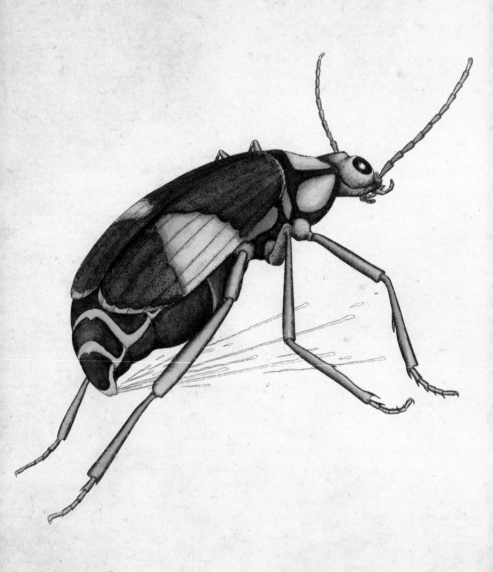

BOMBARDIER BEETLE
Stenaptinus insignis

When Charles Darwin was a young man in college in 1828, he found his passion not in the classroom but in the outdoors. Like many young Englishmen of his day, he was an avid beetle collector. Hunting for bugs in the English countryside may seem like a fairly tame pastime, but Darwin managed to get into trouble—and make an interesting discovery—during one of his field trips. He wrote:

SIZE: Up to ³/₄ in (2 cm)

FAMILY: Carabidae

HABITAT: a variety of habitats, from deserts to forests

DISTRIBUTION: North and South America, Europe, Australia, Middle East, Africa, Asia, and New Zealand

MEET THE RELATIVES: There are over 3000 species in this family, found worldwide.

One day, on tearing off some old bark, I saw two rare beetles, and seized one in each hand; then I saw a third and new kind, which I could not bear to lose, so that I popped the one which I held in my right hand into my mouth. Alas! it ejected some intensely acrid fluid, which burnt my tongue so that I was forced to spit the beetle out, which was lost, as was the third one.

The beetle Darwin placed in his mouth was almost certainly a kind of ground beetle known as a bombardier beetle. Grab one of these insects, and you'll hear a surprisingly loud popping noise just as a hot, stinging spray is ejected from an artillery-like structure on the bug's rear end.

The bombardier beetle poses little threat to humans—except, maybe, collectors who store live insects in their mouths. Its enemies, however—ants, larger beetles, spiders, even frogs and birds—flee in terror when the bombardier takes aim.

The mechanism by which it engages its enemy would fascinate any weapons manufacturer. In one gland, the bombardier stores hydroquinone and hydrogen peroxide. The two don't interact unless they are mixed with a catalyst to accelerate a chemical reaction—and that is exactly what happens when the bombardier comes under attack. The contents of the gland are forced into a reaction chamber and mixed with a catalyst that transforms the chemicals and heats them to the boiling point. The reaction creates enough pressure to force the spray out of the reaction chamber with a loud pop. Sophisticated recordings of this phenomenon show that the insect fires repeatedly, like an automatic weapon, ejecting five hundred to one thousand blasts per second at its attacker.

The insect fires repeatedly, like an automatic weapon, ejecting five hundred to one thousand blasts per second at its attacker.

About five hundred species of bombardier beetles are found throughout the world. In the United States, bombardiers are all members of the *Brachinus* genus. They can be found under boards, bark, and loose rocks, and at night they scramble about in the open, preferring damp areas. Thanks to their elegant defense system, some can live for several years. The African bombardier beetle, *Stenaptinus insignis*, is impressive not only for its bright yellow-and-black markings but also for its ability to swivel its hindquarters up to 270 degrees, allowing it to spray in almost any direction and even knock an attacker off its back.

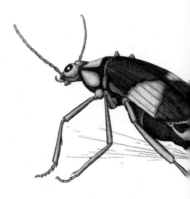

TARANTULA
Theraphosa blondi

SIZE: Up to 12 in (30 cm), including legs

FAMILY: Theraphosidae

HABITAT: Forests, foothills, and deserts, primarily in warm climates

DISTRIBUTION: North and South America, Africa, Asia, Middle East, Australia, New Zealand, and Europe

MEET THE RELATIVES: There are over 800 species of tarantulas worldwide.

Carole Hargis may well be the most inept murderer California has ever seen. In early 1977, she grew disenchanted with her marriage to David Hargis, a Marine Corps drill instructor stationed in San Diego. So she hatched a plan to murder him by baking a tarantula pie. Carole kept a pet tarantula, and at first she considered putting the hairy spider in bed with her husband, hoping he would get bitten. But then she had a better idea. She removed the tarantula's venom sac and hid it in a blackberry pie. Her husband took a few bites but never touched the venom.

Among the many mistakes Carole Hargis made was misunderstanding the lethality of a tarantula's venom. Not that tarantulas aren't intimidating: the largest tarantula, *Theraphosa blondi*, spans almost a foot (thirty centimeters) in length with its legs outstretched. It spins a trap and waits for its prey to walk by—a mouse, perhaps—then it pounces. With fangs almost an inch (two and a half centimeters) in length, it injects its venom and kills the prey. And like some other tarantulas, it is covered in urticating (stinging)

She removed the tarantula's venom sac and hid it in a blackberry pie. Her husband took a few bites but never touched the venom.

hairs, which it can fling at an enemy when threatened.

But despite this fierce behavior, the bite of a tarantula is really no worse than that of a wasp or a bee. It will certainly sting—in fact, scientists recently discovered that the bite of the West Indian tarantula *Psalmopoeus cambridgei* goes to work on nerve cells with the same mechanism employed by habanero peppers. That intense, hot pain is hard to bear but not fatal. For people with severe allergies, the venom can be quite dangerous, though most people will survive it.

In addition to its role in this strange case, the tarantula has long been associated with the Italian tarantella, a folk dance that gets faster and faster as it progresses until it is quite frantic. Tarantism, a kind of dancing mania in southern Italy during the fifteenth, sixteenth, and seventeenth centuries, was believed at the time to have been caused by the bite of a tarantula. But in fact, it was more likely caused by ergot poisoning (a fungus that infects rye), or it could have been the result of some kind of mass anxiety or hysteria. Regardless, it is highly unlikely that the tarantula was to blame.

STINGING CATERPILLARS

When a twenty-two-year-old woman on vacation in Peru returned home to Canada, she found strange bruises on her legs. For four days she watched as they got bigger, not smaller. She was otherwise in perfect health. Her doctor asked if anything unusual had happened during her vacation, and she said that one week earlier, while walking barefoot in Peru, she had stepped on five caterpillars. The pain had been immediate and severe, running up her thigh and making it difficult to walk. She also got a headache. But she felt fine the next day, and it didn't occur to her to see a doctor.

After the woman returned home, the bruises began. Some of them were as large as her hand and getting bigger. Her doctors searched for medical reports of caterpillar stings and realized that a species from Brazil could be to blame. They contacted a hospital there and made arrangements to ship a Brazilian-made antivenin to Canada. It would take two days to arrive.

By the time the antivenin was administered, it had been ten days since the caterpillar stings. The woman's blood wasn't clotting properly, and she died later that day.

Cases of death by caterpillar are extraordinarily rare and limited to just a few known species, but many caterpillars employ painful defenses to protect themselves.

ARCHDUKE CATERPILLAR *Lexias spp.:* These pale green caterpillars, rarely seen except in their native countries in Southeast Asia or on butterfly farms, are covered with exquisitely sharp spines that extend outward like the needles of a pine tree. This thorny armor deters predators and protects the young caterpillars from getting eaten by their siblings as they search for food. The beautiful butterflies that develop are often found in butterfly conservatories and framed butterfly collections. The wings of the adult males are primarily black, with patterns of blue, yellow, or white markings.

FIRE CATERPILLAR *Lonomia obliqua and L. achelous:* These are the species most likely to have killed the Canadian woman. *L. obliqua* is found in southern Brazil, and *L. achelous* in northern Brazil and Venezuela. The green, brown, and white caterpillars are covered in sharp hairs that resemble cactus spines. The small creatures tend to mass together on the ground or on the trunk of a tree, so it's possible to be stung by several at once by walking barefoot or leaning against a tree. The caterpillars release a powerful toxin that causes massive internal bleeding and organ failure. Although the antivenin developed in Brazil is effective, it should be administered within twenty-four hours. It's critical to seek immediate medical attention.

Brazilian scientists believe that deforestation is bringing more people into contact with the caterpillar. As the jungle trees it prefers get cut down, the caterpillar moves into more populated areas. Over the past decade, public health officials have recorded 444 *Lonomia* stings. Seven resulted in death.

GYPSY MOTH CATERPILLAR *Lymantria dispar:* In the spring of 1981, roughly a third of children at two schools in Pennsylvania suffered from rashes on their arms, necks, and legs. Doctors took scrapings and throat cultures to test for infection, but found nothing. Finally, they interviewed the children, both who had a rash and who didn't, about the amount of time they spent playing in the woods. They found a high correlation between outdoor play and the outbreak of this mysterious rash. They concluded that the rash had been caused by the gypsy moth caterpillar, which was present in high concentrations around the schools.

The rash caused by the long, silky hairs of this caterpillar can be painful, but isn't known to cause long-term harm. The caterpillars, however, do significant damage to forests. While the caterpillars may not kill the trees, they weaken them enough to allow diseases to take hold. Over the past thirty years, over a million acres of hardwood forests have been defoliated (lost their leaves) every year. The caterpillar and its adult form, the gypsy moth, are both found in Canada, and in the United States.

IO MOTH CATERPILLAR *Automeris io:* The io moth is a familiar creature in its native range, which extends from Canada's southern

Ontario, Quebec, and New Brunswick down through North and South Dakota, into Arizona, New Mexico, and Texas, and east to Florida. The moths have large spots resembling eyes on their lower wings, making them a popular subject for nature photographers. But the caterpillars are fascinating as well—and fearsome. These pale green creatures are covered with fleshy nodules, and from each nodule sprouts a cluster of stinging, black-tipped spines. The sting is painful but harmless, although allergic reactions can be severe and may require medical attention.

PUSS CATERPILLAR *Megalopyge opercularis:* This caterpillar looks like a tiny Persian cat. The so-called flannel moth or asp moth is one of the most toxic caterpillars in North America. Anyone who rubs up against its long, silky golden-brown hairs will find those hairs embedded under the skin, where they cause burning pain, a rash, and blisters. The pain can radiate up a limb, and the most extreme reactions can also include nausea, swollen lymph nodes, and respiratory distress. Most people recover in a day, but in the worst cases, it may take several days for symptoms to subside. People who have been stung say that the pain was like "my arm had been broken" or like "a hammer hit me."

Don't be fooled that this caterpillar looks like a tiny Persian cat.

There is no specific treatment to soothe the pain, other than ice packs, antihistamines, or creams and ointments. The hairs can sometimes be pulled out by applying tape to the skin, but even removing them may offer little relief. The caterpillars are found throughout the southern United States in late spring and early summer. The adults, which emerge later in the summer, are also extremely fuzzy, resembling large, furry bees.

THE ANTS GO MARCHING

nts are incredibly useful, acting as "shredders" to break down organic matter and recycle nutrients back into the soil, as well as serving as a food source for other small creatures in the food chain. They are also a marvel of social organization, maintaining complex colonies with divisions of labor, sophisticated communication, and the remarkable ability to act as a group to carry out their missions. They wage war, maintain farms of fungus, and build intricate nests with chambers for day-care centers while also performing other functions important to the community. But the behavior of some ants is not just fascinating—it's terrifying and, in some cases, brilliantly painful.

ARGENTINE ANT *Linepithema humile:* This tiny, dark brown ant species probably slipped into New Orleans in the 1890s on board a coffee ship coming from Latin America. The mild and damp coastal climate proved so favorable that the ants spread across the Southeast and west to California. Citrus farmers sounded the alarm as early as 1908, but their attempts at controlling this invasive ant proved ineffective. The Argentine ant's ability to form "supercolonies" that span hundreds of miles sounds like something right out of a horror movie.

These ants, just one-tenth of an inch (three millimeters) long, are surprisingly aggressive. They don't sting or bite people, but they have wiped out colonies of native ants that are ten times their size. The loss of those native ants means the disappearance of a food source for creatures higher up the food chain, including California's coastal

Entomologists now realize that the population of Argentine ants that extends from San Diego into Northern California is one giant supercolony of genetically similar ants.

horned lizard; it has not only lost its favorite food source but also must face attacks from swarms of Argentine ants.

But the Argentine ant's favorite food source is not other ants. It is actually honeydew—not the melon but the sweet secretions of aphids and juice-sucking insects called scale. To make sure that these pests produce enough honeydew, the ants protect them while they do their damage to rosebushes, citrus trees, and other plants. They even carry the pests around to make sure they find enough to eat.

The disruption caused by these ants, which can exist by the millions under just one single-family home, is almost impossible to fathom. They have driven other ants, termites, wasps, bees, and even birds from their nests, and caused damage to agricultural crops. They act in an incredibly organized, militaristic fashion, never going to war with one another, always working together to accomplish their mission.

In fact, entomologists now realize that the population of Argentine ants that extends from San Diego into Northern California is one giant supercolony of genetically similar ants. A European colony extends all along the Mediterranean coast, and supercolonies in Australia and Japan are also well established. The members of all these colonies are so closely related, and so unwilling to fight one another, that they can almost be thought of as one global megacolony acting as a single entity to carry out its mission.

BULLET ANT *Paraponera clavata:* The bullet ant gets its name from the fact that its bite feels like a gunshot. Those who have had the misfortune of getting bitten by this inch-long (two and a half centimeters) South American ant say that the pain is overpowering for several hours, then subsides over the next few days. Some people are temporarily unable to use the limb that's been stung, and some report nausea, sweating, and shaking after the attack.

British naturalist and television star Steve Backshall deliberately braved the sting of the bullet ant when he was filming a documentary in Brazil. He joined members of the Sateré-Mawé tribe in a male initiation ritual that involved being stung continuously by a swarm of ants for ten minutes. The pain left him screaming, crying, and writhing on the ground. Soon, he was drooling and nearly unresponsive, thanks to the powerful neurotoxins in the venom. "If there'd been a machete to hand," he told reporters, "I'd have chopped off my arms to escape the pain."

DRIVER ANT *Dorylus sp.:* When driver ants are hungry, they hit the road. In leaderless swarms, they stream through villages in Central and East Africa, decimating everything in their path. As many as twenty million ants join the swarm, enough to build tunnels as they go and overpower grasshoppers, worms, beetles, and even larger creatures like snakes and rats. Because these inch-long (two and a half centimeters) ants barrel right through villages and homes, people may be forced to move out during the onslaught. This is not always such a bad thing—the ants wipe out cockroaches, scorpions, and other household pests during their march.

In 2009, an archaeologist exhuming the bodies of Rwandan gorillas to do research on evolution woke up one morning to find a river of driver ants streaming through the excavation site. "Just so you know," said one of her colleagues, "this day is going to suck." The scientists donned protective gear and tried to stay as far away from the swarm as possible. By the end of the day, the ants had eaten their fill and moved on. When the team returned to the dig, they realized that the driver ants had done them a favor by removing every other bug from the soil, allowing them to retrieve clean, intact skeletons.

FIRE ANT *Solenopsis invicta:* Also known as the red imported fire ant, this South American native forms colonies of up to 250,000 members that feed on aphid secretions, as well as dead animals, worms, and other insects. They can take over the nests of birds and rodents, devour the shoots of crops like soybeans and corn, and even disable farm equipment.

Their ability to tamper with mechanical and electrical systems is particularly frustrating. They chew on the insulation around wiring, switches, and controls, resulting in tractors that won't start, electrical circuits that short out, and air conditioners that won't operate. They have even disabled traffic lights. In all, the damage caused by fire ants in the United States exceeds $2 billion per year.

But most people fear the fire ant for its vicious sting. Roughly a third to a half of all people living in the fire ant's path—an area extending from New Mexico to North Carolina—get bitten every year. When fire ants attack, usually in response to someone accidentally stumbling into a colony, they bite hard, then inject their venom, causing immediate pain at the site of the sting. If the ant isn't knocked off, it will sting a few more times in the same area. These stings raise a red welt with a white pustule in the center.

Attempts to control fire ants have been expensive, time-consuming, and ineffective.

A severe attack, and the scratching that often follows it, can introduce infection and leave scars. People working on construction or landscaping crews risk getting hundreds of bites at once when they stumble upon a colony—perhaps resulting in extreme swelling of an arm or a leg, which can last a month or longer. In 2006, a South Carolina woman died from such an attack while gardening. She experienced the same kind of anaphylactic shock that sometimes affects people after bee stings.

Attempts to control fire ants have been expensive, time-consuming, and ineffective. Chemical sprays only wiped out the competition, making it easier for fire ants to get established. Now authorities in Australia are actually hunting them by helicopter, using heat-sensing equipment to locate their enormous mounds so that pesticides can be injected directly into the ants' homes.

SCHMIDT STING PAIN INDEX

Justin Schmidt, an entomologist who studies venomous stings, created the Schmidt Sting Pain Index to quantify the pain inflicted by ants and other stinging creatures. The scale begins at 0 for painless stings and goes up to 4 for the most painful stings imaginable. How does he know? He's been stung by over 150 insects while doing research.

1.0 SWEAT BEE: Light, ephemeral, almost fruity. A tiny spark has singed a single hair on your arm.

1.2 FIRE ANT: Sharp, sudden, mildly alarming. Like walking across a shag carpet and reaching for the light switch.

1.8 BULLHORN ACACIA ANT: A rare, piercing, elevated sort of pain. Someone has fired a staple into your cheek.

2.0 BALD-FACED HORNET: Rich, hearty, slightly crunchy. Similar to getting your hand mashed in a revolving door.

2.0 YELLOWJACKET: Hot and smoky, almost irreverent. Imagine someone extinguishing a cigar on your tongue.

2.X HONEYBEE AND EUROPEAN HORNET: Like a match head that flips off and burns on your skin.

3.0 RED HARVESTER ANT: Bold and unrelenting. Somebody is using a drill to excavate your ingrown toenail.

3.0 PAPER WASP: Caustic and burning. Distinctly bitter aftertaste. Like spilling a beaker of hydrochloric acid on a paper cut.

4.0 TARANTULA HAWK: Blinding, fierce, shockingly electric. A running hair dryer has been dropped into your bubble bath.

4.0+ BULLET ANT: Pure, intense, brilliant pain. Like fire-walking over flaming charcoal with a 3-inch rusty nail in your heel.

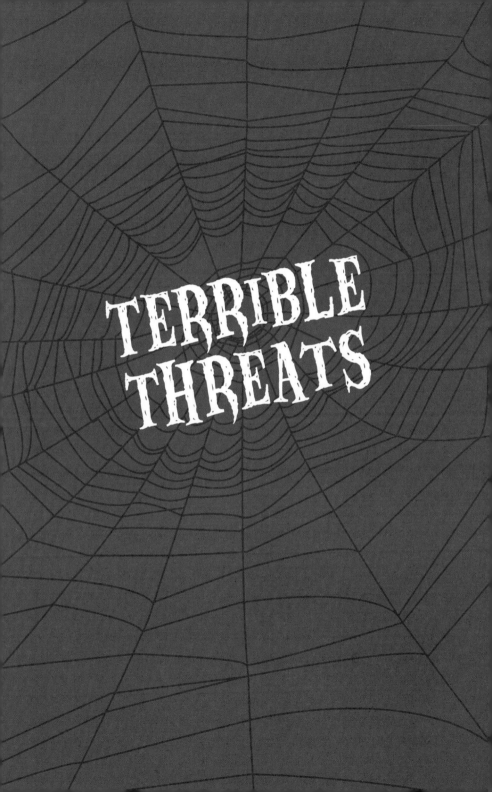

TERRIBLE THREATS

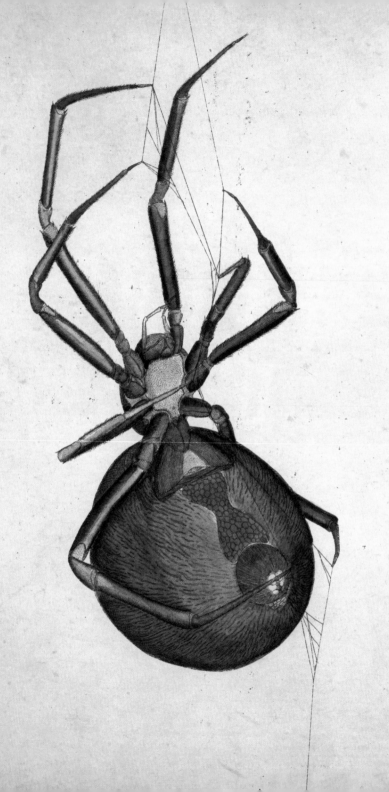

BLACK WIDOW
Latrodectus hesperus

SIZE: 1½ in (3.8 cm), including legs

FAMILY: Theridiidae

HABITAT: Dark, secluded areas, including logs and rock piles, under shrubs and trees, and around woodpiles, sheds, barns, and cellars

DISTRIBUTION: Nearly worldwide; North and South America, Africa, the Middle East, Europe, Asia, Australia, and New Zealand

MEET THE RELATIVES: About thirty species of venomous spiders make up the *Latrodectus* genus. They are part of a large and diverse family of spiders known as cobweb or tangle-web spiders.

"To whom it may concern," wrote twenty-six-year-old Stephen Liarsky in his suicide note. "Whenever a man usually takes his life it is always proper to give the reason. My reason is because, first, I have no job. I have no one in this world except a woman I love terribly, and she is too good for me. I am ashamed of myself because I am a failure and not a success. God bless Rose. Good-bye."

This 1935 suicide was unusual not so much for its motive but for its method—a black widow spider bite. The spider was found in a cardboard box under Mr. Liarsky's bed, along with paperwork indicating that he had purchased her from California with assurances that her bite was fatal and incurable.

He died two days later. Hospital officials found a bottle of sleeping pills under his pillow and ruled that the pills, not the spider, were to blame for his death. But it was too late. By that time, the

During World War II, the London Zoo killed its black widow spiders, along with other venomous insects and snakes, as a precaution against the possibility of their being liberated during air raids.

so-called Black Widow Suicide had attracted nationwide attention. Several high-profile reports of black widow deaths started appearing in the news. An investigative reporter in Texas tried to prove that suicide by black widow was impossible by attempting (unsuccessfully) to persuade a black widow to bite him. A committee was formed in Oklahoma to eliminate the spider from the state for the sake of protecting the children. During World War II, the London Zoo killed its black widow spiders, along with other venomous insects and snakes, as a precaution against the possibility of their being liberated during air raids.

The black widow is perhaps the best-known and most widely feared spider in the world. About forty species can be found around the world in North and South America, Africa, Australia, and Europe. The female's round, black body is usually (but not always) marked by a distinctive red hourglass shape on the abdomen. The males—small, light brown creatures that bear little resemblance to their wives—don't bite at all, making them more of an afterthought in the story of these frightful creatures.

Although the spider gets its name from the belief that the females always eat the males after mating, this behavior is seen most often in the Australian species, the redback spider, or *Latrodectus hasselti*.

Black widows are not particularly eager to bite people; they prefer to use their fangs to go after other insects, which they inject with their own digestive juices, turning their prey to mush and making it easy to drink them down. If they are provoked into biting a person, they inject a tiny bit of venom under the skin, which may cause a pinprick of pain or no pain at all. It isn't until the venom makes its way to the nervous system that trouble begins. The toxin in a black widow's venom will cause a kind of painful storm in the nervous system, bringing on muscle pain and cramps. People may get shaky and dizzy, and feel their heart race or slow dangerously. Some people experience sweating, especially around the site of the bite. Doctors call this syndrome latrodectism, after the spider's scientific name.

The bite is rarely fatal, but bite victims are encouraged to seek treatment for the symptoms, which can be painful and debilitating. In severe cases, victims may receive an antivenin made from the blood serum of horses that has been injected with black widow venom. This venom can be obtained only by "milking" live black widow spiders, a laborious process that involves giving the spiders a mild electrical shock that induces them to eject venom, which is then vacuumed into a narrow tube. The spider often vomits as a result of the electrical shock, making it necessary to set up a dual vacuum system to separate the vomit from the venom as both spew forth from the spider's mouth.

Black widows do tend to bite when they feel trapped. In the days of outdoor privies, spiders hiding under a toilet seat would attack anything that appeared to block their exit. Fortunately, the introduction of indoor plumbing made these excruciating bites in the most sensitive of locations a thing of the past.

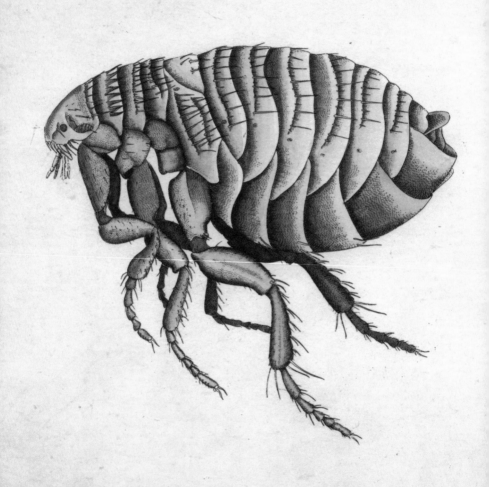

CHIGOE FLEA

Tunga penetrans

SIZE: 1/32 in (1 mm)

FAMILY: Tungidae

HABITAT: Favors sandy, warm soil on deserts and beaches.

DISTRIBUTION: Tropical regions around the world, including Latin America, India, Africa, and the Caribbean.

MEET THE RELATIVES: These fleas are related to other tiny fleas that infest birds and mammals, primarily in South America.

On Christopher Columbus's second voyage to the New World, he established a colony on the island of Hispaniola, which is now home to Haiti and the Dominican Republic. Among the many problems he and his crew faced—a lack of supplies, food shortages, and battles with the local population—nothing was as troublesome as one small sand flea.

Describing Columbus's voyages about thirty years later, Francisco de Oviedo wrote about the troubles that Columbus and his crew suffered. Oviedo explained that the flea burrows under toenails and lays eggs there, creating what he described as "a small sack the size of a lentil, and sometimes like a garbanzo." He noted, "Many lost their feet because of the chigoe. Or at least a few toes . . . because it was necessary to cure themselves with iron or fire." We can only assume that he meant that men in Columbus's crew cut off their own toes, so desperate were they to rid themselves of this terrible infestation.

A female chigoe flea burrows into the skin of her host by simply tearing into it, then living under the skin and dining on the host's blood until she swells to about the size of a pea. She does not allow her host's skin to heal over, maintaining an open wound so that she can breathe. Sometimes, her rear end can be seen in the center of the wound as a tiny black dot. She lays about a hundred eggs over the next week or two. While those eggs will eventually make their way to the sandy beach the flea came from, they tend to stick to the wound—a truly appalling sight. Clusters of tiny white eggs cling to festering wounds. If left untreated, the eggs will eventually drop to the ground. After about a month, the female will die and fall out of the wound as well—but not before creating serious problems for the host.

Men in Columbus's crew cut off their own toes, so desperate were they to rid themselves of this terrible infestation.

Tourists who get infested with the flea on some tropical beach usually do not experience this entire life cycle. They notice a lesion on their foot and get right to a doctor. The doctor carefully cleans it up and removes the flea before she lays eggs. But in poorer communities, people may live with dozens of these lesions on their feet, resulting in chronic infections, gangrene, and even the loss of toes. Because the fleas infest both humans and animals, people who live in close contact with rodents and livestock face far more infestations than tourists strolling on the beach.

One recent study at a slum in northeast Brazil showed that about a third of the residents in the impoverished community were infested with the fleas, a condition called tungiasis. Some people had over a hundred lesions on their feet, hands, and chest. The infestations were so bad that many of them had trouble walking or gripping anything with their hands. They had lost fingernails and toenails entirely. The researchers made a point of mentioning that local doctors did not observe or treat parasites like the chigoe flea unless they were specifically asked about it. While the idea of a doctor overlooking dozens of sores oozing the eggs of parasites seems unimaginable, it demonstrates how common the infestation is. Treatment for people participating in the study consisted of a simple cleaning, a tube of ointment, and the gift of a pair of tennis shoes to each patient.

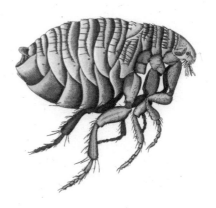

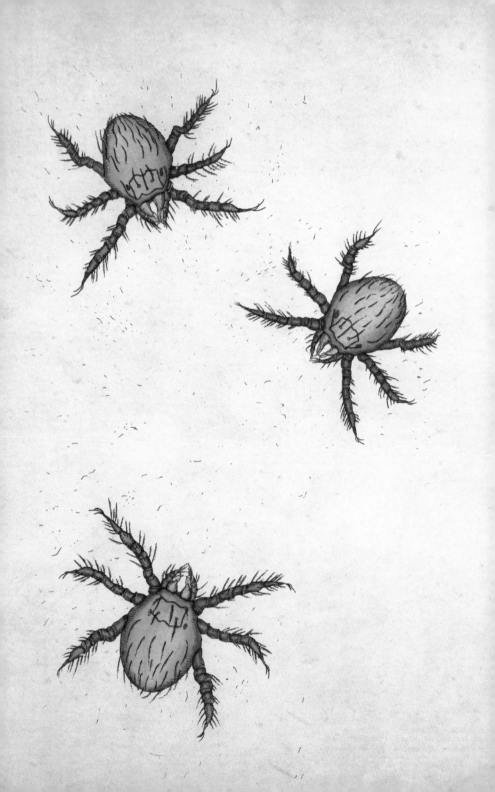

CHIGGER MITE
Leptotrombidium sp.

Soldiers fighting in World War II had to face down more than the enemy. In Burma, monsoon weather, unfamiliar terrain, and exotic diseases made for a deadly combination. Virtually every soldier in the area was hospitalized at some point during 1944. Soldiers were nineteen times more likely to die from disease than from battle wounds. Hepatitis, malaria, and dysentery posed serious problems, but perhaps the most challenging disease was the unfamiliar and unpredictable scrub typhus. The illness was transmitted by a tiny arachnid known as a chigger mite.

SIZE: 0.4 mm

FAMILY: Trombiculidae

HABITAT: Low-lying, damp grasslands and woodlands

DISTRIBUTION: Throughout Asia and Australia

MEET THE RELATIVES: Members of this family include harvest mites and other tiny bloodsucking creatures. The larvae of many species of mites may be referred to as chiggers, but so-called chiggers found in the United States are usually young harvest mites that do not transmit disease.

The chigger, actually the larval form of a mite in the genus *Leptotrombidium*, is a minute creature that feeds on blood only once in its life. It is so small that its mouth can't even penetrate the skin deeply enough to hit a blood vessel. It simply bites into the skin and drinks down a kind of liquefied beverage of skin tissue and blood. A person may not even feel the bite until later, when a little redness develops at the site. This is usually caused by the chigger leaving its feeding tube behind, which can irritate the skin the way a tiny splinter would. Once the chigger has enjoyed its one and only blood meal, it matures into an adult mite and feeds only on plants for the rest of its life.

How, then, is the chigger mite able to transmit disease? If it feeds only once, there is no opportunity to take up the infection from one host and pass it on to another. Scientists solved this mystery when they were able to prove in the laboratory that these mites are capable of trans-ovarial transmission. In other words, adult chiggers that get infected during their one blood meal then pass the infection on to their offspring. For that reason, a young chigger may already be infected from birth, and pass the infection on when it takes its first and only blood meal.

One army medical expert who treated the disease predicted that all his patients infected with scrub typhus would live with permanent heart damage.

Scrub typhus, also called tsutsugamushi fever, is found in populations of wild rats, voles, mice, birds, and also in humans. People who have been infected with the *Orientia tsutsugamushi* bacteria usually experience flu-like symptoms after about ten days, including muscle aches, swollen lymph nodes, fever, and loss of appetite. Eventually, the disease can move into the heart, lung, and kidneys, resulting in death if antibiotics and other lifesaving treatments are not administered in time. Up to a third of people who don't get treatment will die from the disease.

During World War II, scrub typhus was frustratingly hard to avoid in Burma. The mites lived in tall kunai grass, which grows to ten to twenty feet (three to six meters). Soldiers had no choice but to march through it. Burning down the fields of grass might have eliminated the mites, but this wasn't always feasible in a war zone. The clothing the soldiers wore could hardly be sealed tightly enough to keep these tiny mites away. Soldiers who came down with the disease lost, on average, a hundred days of combat duty. By comparison, they typically lost only fourteen days for malaria cases. Twenty percent of them developed pneumonia, and one army medical expert who treated the disease predicted that all his patients infected with scrub typhus would live with permanent heart damage.

Today, scrub typhus infections still occur in parts of Australia, Japan, China, Southeast Asia, the Pacific Islands, and Sri Lanka. There is no vaccine available, and over a million people are infected worldwide.

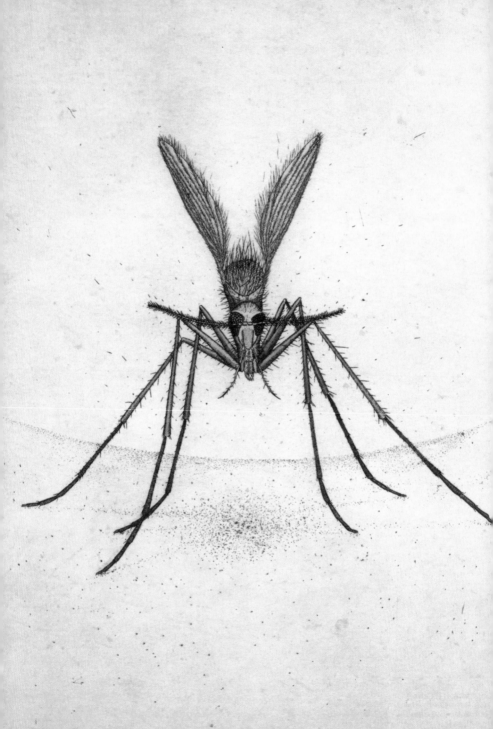

SAND FLY
Phlebotomus *sp.*

B ritish television personality Ben Fogle has had plenty of opportunities to be exposed to dreadful exotic diseases. The host of BBC adventure programs *Castaway 2000*, *Extreme Dreams*, and *Wild in Africa* has trekked through Central and South America, been marooned on a remote island in the Outer Hebrides, crossed the Atlantic in a rowboat, and raced across the Sahara Desert on foot. He was, it seemed, invincible—until, at the age of thirty-four, he met the sand fly.

SIZE: Up to 1/8 in (3 mm)

FAMILY: Psychodidae

HABITAT: Forests, wooded wetlands, and sandy areas near water sources in tropical and subtropical climates

DISTRIBUTION: *Phlebotomus* species in the Middle East, southern parts of Europe, and in parts of Asia and Africa; sand flies in the genus *Lutzomyia* (which also transmit leishmaniasis) in many parts of Latin America

MEET THE RELATIVES: There are dozens of species of these bloodsucking flies that transmit disease, but the insect most Americans refer to as a sand fly is actually a more distant relative called a biting midge.

This tiny wheat-colored fly lives for only two weeks as an adult. The females require blood meals to nurture their eggs, and while their bites may be almost painless, they can be extremely annoying. In sand fly–infested areas, people often find themselves in the middle of a swarm. This happens because the males, which don't bite, hang around warm-blooded hosts waiting for a female to show up for dinner. So what may feel like an attack is actually an elaborate mating ritual that just happens to have a food source at the center of it—you. Entomologists call this swarm a mating lek.

When a female bites, she injects her mouthparts into the skin, using her toothed mandibles like scissors so that she can create a pool of blood to drink. She injects an anticlotting substance that allows her to enjoy her meal a little longer. The flies transmit several diseases, but perhaps the best known is leishmaniasis. This is the disease that nearly killed Ben Fogle after an expedition through Peru.

Fogle began to feel some malaria-like symptoms while he was in the jungle—dizziness, headaches, lack of appetite—but he continued filming, then returned to London to train for an expedition to the South Pole. He collapsed during training and was bedridden for weeks while doctors tried to make a diagnosis. Tests for malaria and other, better-known diseases were negative. It wasn't until an ugly sore erupted on his arm that he finally had a clue.

The less harmful cutaneous form of the disease is such a problem in the Middle East that troops stationed there refer to it as Baghdad Boil.

Leishmaniasis is caused by parasitic protozoa, a single-celled organism, transmitted from other animals to humans via the bite of the sand fly. The disease takes different forms: cutaneous leishmaniasis, which causes a sore that can take months or even a year to heal, and visceral leishmaniasis, a potentially fatal version in which the protozoa infest the internal organs. Another form, mucocutaneous leishmaniasis, causes ulcers and long-lasting damage around the nose and mouth. Fogle had the misfortune to be infected with the more dangerous form of the disease. He required long-term intravenous treatment, followed by another round of treatment after he suffered a relapse while on his South Pole expedition. He's now back at work writing, traveling, and filming new shows.

The less harmful cutaneous form of the disease is such a problem in the Middle East that troops stationed there refer to it as Baghdad Boil. In 1991, U.S. soldiers returning from the Gulf War were asked not to donate blood for two years due to the possibility of transmitting leishmaniasis. There was another outbreak in 2003. Although military officials issued warnings about the threat, bug sprays and bed nets were not always available, and troops may not have understood the seriousness of the threat. It is now estimated that over two thousand troops have been infected, but the number could be significantly higher because troops are treated in the field rather than flown to military hospitals where statistics are kept. Unfortunately, doctors in the United States may not recognize the skin lesions since the disease is not common here—and that could lead to misdiagnoses and delays in treatment for returning soldiers.

Around the world, an estimated 1.5 million people become infected with the cutaneous form of the disease every year, and half a million are diagnosed with the more dangerous visceral form. The drugs used to treat the disease are themselves quite serious and require close monitoring by a doctor. Although research on a vaccine is underway, the only way to prevent the disease right now is to avoid the sand fly—which, despite its name, is found not just in desert climates as in Iraq but throughout the tropics and subtropics.

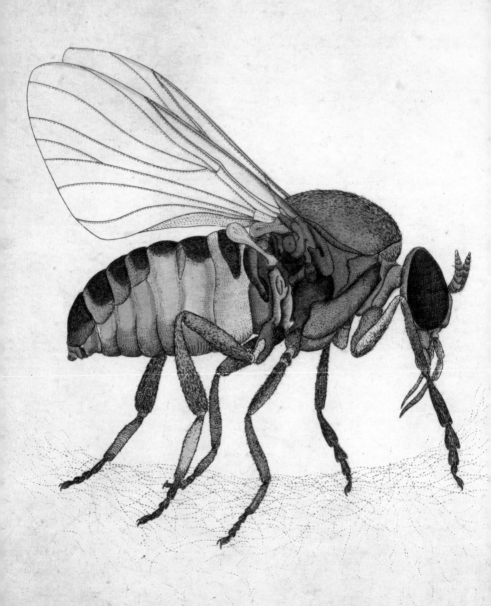

BLACK FLY
Simulium damnosum

Fewer than fifty years ago, a third of villagers living alongside West African rivers could expect to be blind by the time they reached adulthood. The blame for this tragedy rests with the black fly, called one of "the world's most persistent and demoralizing man-biting insect pests" by a leading medical entomologist. Eventually, those areas had to be abandoned, a terrible decision for people who depended on the rich soil for agriculture.

SIZE: 1/16– 3/16 in (2–5 mm)

FAMILY: Simuliidae

HABITAT: Near fast-moving streams

DISTRIBUTION: Various species throughout the United States and Canada, as well as across Europe, Russia, and Africa

MEET THE RELATIVES: Although there are over 700 species of black flies worldwide, only 10 to 20 percent are pests to humans or animals. They don't all transmit disease, but they are an incredible nuisance, interfering with tourism and outdoor enterprises, like logging and farming, throughout the summer months.

Female black flies lay their eggs on the surface of fast-moving rivers, where the water has the high oxygen content their young require. The eggs hatch and the larvae linger along the river for a week before they emerge as fully formed adults. The females mate immediately and only once. After that, they desperately seek out a warm-blooded creature to feed on. The only way they can get enough nutrition to nurture their eggs is by drinking the blood of a human or an animal. They will live for a month, laying their eggs in the river to perpetuate the cycle. Some rivers can produce one billion flies per kilometer of riverbed in a single day.

A person under attack in an area of heavy infestation may expect to get hundreds of bites in an hour! In some cases, they swarm so densely—climbing into the ears, nose, eyes, and mouth—that an animal can suffocate or run itself off a cliff in an attempt to get away. The flies have even killed livestock by exsanguination, or the draining of blood. During a massive attack, the shock to the system from the various compounds found in their saliva, a condition called simuliotoxicosis, can also kill an animal. In 1923, along Europe's Danube River, a ferocious swarm left twenty-two thousand animals dead.

 In 1923, along Europe's Danube River in the southern Carpathian Mountains, a ferocious swarm left twenty-two thousand animals dead.

The most remarkable fact of the black fly's short, bloodthirsty life is that if it feasts on the blood of a person infected with a parasitic nematode (a cylindrical worm) called *Onchocerca volvulus*, it takes part in a intricate cycle of disease transmission.

The young nematodes—called microfilariae during their early larval stage—cannot grow and develop while they are swimming in the bloodstream of a human. They must be sucked into the body of a black fly to grow into their next larval stage. They enter the black fly while the fly feeds. There they move into its saliva and wait for it to feed again—because only by moving back into the body of a human can the worm continue its journey to adulthood.

If they successfully navigate this complicated voyage from human to fly and back to human, the microfilariae finally transform into adult nematodes that can reach over a foot (thirty centimeters) in length. These adults nestle into masses under a person's skin, where they live for up to fifteen years, mating and producing as many as a thousand offspring per day.

Most of these offspring will never be lucky enough to find their way into the gut of a black fly, which means that they will be doomed to swim around the human body in their juvenile state for a year or two until they die—but not before inflicting terrible symptoms on their host. They burrow into the eyes, where they cause blindness. The skin gets depigmented and breaks out in rashes and lesions. The tiny creatures itch so horribly that people break their skin open with sticks and rocks in a futile attempt to scratch the irritation away. This, in turn, causes bacterial infections, making sleep impossible, and has even driven some to suicide.

Today, twenty-five million people are infected worldwide. Of those, three hundred thousand are blind and eight hundred thousand live with severe vision impairment. One approach to controlling the disease is to kill the black fly, and that worked through the 1950s when DDT, a chemical pesticide, was available. But the flies became resistant to DDT, and DDT itself accumulated in the food chain at toxic levels. Now a particular strain of a natural bacterium is used in its place, but this provides no treatment for the millions affected by the disease.

A dewormer for animals called ivermectin has proven effective against the microfilariae, but not the adult worms. Its manufacturer, Merck, provides the drug free of charge to public health groups, which distribute annual treatments to infected people. When the adult worms eventually die—which can take over a decade—the treatment can stop, but in the meantime, the repeated doses are necessary to keep the young worms in check and prevent transmission of the disease. The program has been so successful that abandoned river valleys are being resettled, and distribution of the drug is beginning in other African and Latin American countries.

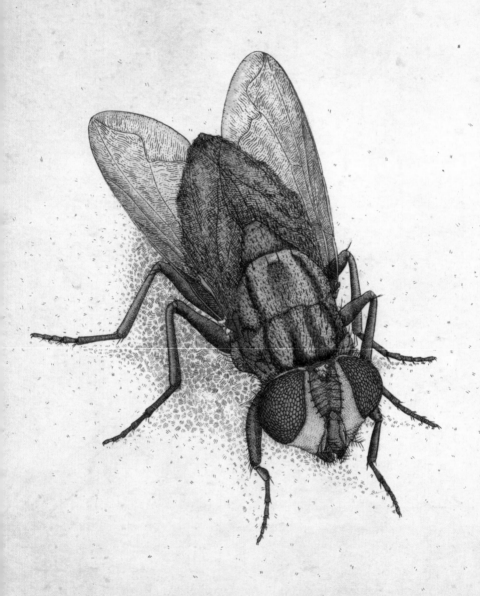

FILTH FLY
Musca sorbens

SIZE: $1/4$–$5/16$ in (6–8 mm)

FAMILY: Muscidae

HABITAT: Decaying organic matter, including sewage, garbage, dead animals, and other waste

DISTRIBUTION: In warmer climates worldwide, particularly in areas of human habitation

MEET THE RELATIVES: This family of flies includes the common house fly, Musca domestica, and stable flies.

New York City's Randall's Island served as a "house of refuge" for juvenile delinquents from 1854 until it was closed in 1935. Boys and girls ages eight to seventeen detained there were put to work making hoop skirts, shoes, chair frames, sieves, and rattraps. The girls did cooking, housework, and laundry, and made all the uniforms for the inmates. A half hour to an hour per day was devoted to schooling. Punishments for bad behavior included being sent to bed without supper, a bread-and-water diet, solitary confinement, and beatings. Although the young people slept in cells, administrators in 1860 thought it might be better to house them in hammocks in open rooms, where constant monitoring could prevent "indulgence in solitary vice."

The young people did not enjoy this treatment. They responded with outbreaks of violence against the staff and attempts to jump into the East River and swim away. The situation got particularly bad in 1897, when an inspection revealed a sewage system that emitted "offensive odors" and an outbreak of a terrible eye disease called trachoma. Roughly 10 percent of the inmates were infected every year. At the time, the connection between these two problems may not have been clear—but it is now.

Trachoma was once a common illness in the United States. It was frequently seen among immigrants attempting to enter through Ellis Island. It is now almost unheard of in wealthy countries, but is all too common in areas of extreme poverty, refugee camps, and prisons throughout the world.

The bacterium that causes trachoma triggers an inflammation of the upper eyelid, which can lead to a cycle of swelling and scarring that shortens the inner lining. Eventually, the eyelashes pull into the eye itself. This incredibly painful condition, called trichiasis, leads to damage to the cornea and vision problems. If left untreated, a person can go blind.

Right now, eighty-four million people are infected with the disease, and eight million are losing their sight. It is found in parts of Central and South America, Africa, the Middle East, Asia, and Australia. Antibiotics can treat the infection, and a corneal transplant can treat vision impairment, but these options are often not available in poorer countries. The disease is particularly debilitating in poorer locales for women, who cannot cook over a fire or work in the fields with this condition. Thus, women depend on children—usually girls—to stay home and help them rather than go to school. In some cases, women who suffer the disease are abandoned by their husbands.

While the disease can be spread through close contact, especially between mother and child, health officials also lay the blame squarely on *Musca sorbens*, a relative to the common house fly that has earned the unflattering name "filth fly." This insect swarms around latrines, garbage, and manure piles, then moves bacteria around by picking them up on its hairy legs.

Basic sanitation, such as hand washing and the use of clean cloths to wash children's faces, can slow the spread of the disease, but eliminating the filth fly is a bigger battle. In areas with open latrines and garbage piles, the flies are so thick that people quickly

Soldiers in Vietnam reported that the flies were so thick in the mess halls that it was impossible not to eat a few of them with their meals.

give up on swatting them away and spend their days with flies climbing in and out of their noses, mouths, and eyes. Soldiers in Vietnam reported that the flies were so thick in the mess halls that it was impossible not to eat a few of them with their meals.

The solution lies in the construction of latrines designed to keep flies out. One design, called a ventilated improved pit latrine, or VIP, is seen by public health organizations as one of the best approaches to keeping the filth fly out of people's lives. It features a vent pipe covered with a screen to keep flies out. The vent also catches wind currents and uses them for circulation, lifting odors away. A representative of former president Jimmy Carter's foundation, the Carter Center, recently announced that it had hoped to install ten thousand VIPs in Ethiopia, but villagers were so taken with the idea that they installed *ninety* thousand. Looking back to Carter's childhood, the spokesman said, "They look just like the outhouses people in Georgia were using 50 years ago."

I'VE GOT YOU UNDER MY SKIN

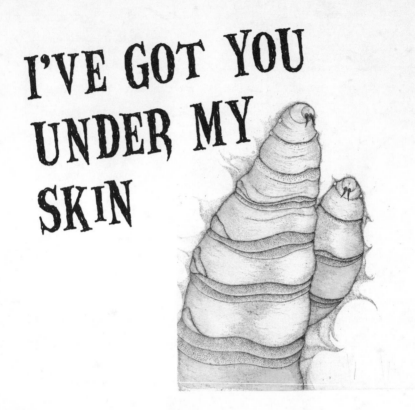

Nobody loves a maggot. Even the name elicits a shudder of disgust.

These white, wormy creatures are nothing more than baby flies, and no more or less grotesque than any other insect's offspring. They usually cluster around some food source their mother has found for them, and they're doing nothing but eating and growing as children should. What's so offensive about that?

Nothing—except when the thing they are eating is *us*.

CONGO FLOOR MAGGOT *Auchmeromyia senegalensis:* Found south of the Sahara, the Congo floor maggot flies like to lay their eggs on the warm, dry floors of huts or in caves and barns where animals are sheltered. When the larvae hatch, they wander around on the floor at night, looking for a warm-blooded creature to feed on. They will bite humans in the night and drink their blood for about twenty minutes at a time. Although they inflict painful, swollen bites, they don't transmit disease or burrow under the skin. People who sleep on mats are unable to avoid being bitten, but those lucky enough to sleep in a bed are rarely bothered by these nighttime bloodsuckers.

HUMAN BOT FLY *Dermatobia hominis:* Travelers returning from Mexico and Central America sometimes come home with more than a souvenir T-shirt. The human bot fly can hitch a ride with tourists, making itself known only when a sore resembling an insect bite doesn't get better.

This fly has an ingenious method of getting under people's skin. It can crawl right into an open wound, but an even more effective strategy is to capture a mosquito, lay eggs on the mosquito, and let it go off in search of a warm-blooded human. The eggs may simply fall off the mosquito when it lands on an arm or a leg, or they may hatch at the moment the mosquito makes contact, enlivened by the warmth of the human host. As the eggs hatch, the larvae crawl right off the mosquito and into the wound it has created. And if there is no mosquito available, a bot fly will happily use a tick for transportation, instead.

If left undisturbed, the larvae will settle under the skin and feed for two to three months before emerging on their own to drop to the ground and mature. But most people, when confronted with a wound that never quite heals and the uncomfortable feeling that something is moving around under the skin, will not leave it undisturbed. The wound can be painful and itchy, it can ooze a foul-smelling liquid, and some people even claim they can hear the creature moving around. Luckily, these wounds rarely become infected, thanks to an antibacterial secretion from the larva itself.

Extraction of a bot fly larva is not always easy, depending on the location of the bite and the overall health of the human host. Some people are sent home and told to wait it out, which can be intolerable for all but the most entomologically curious. Some try to smother the fly by covering the wound with tape, nail polish, or petroleum jelly, hoping to weaken the larva and pull it out more easily. Doctors have used a simple first aid tool called a venom extractor to remove the creature, and a surgical extraction is sometimes possible, as long as the entire larva can be cleanly removed. One home remedy is to leave a piece of raw bacon over the wound, the theory being that the maggot would prefer bacon to human flesh and would leave voluntarily for this new food source.

SCREW-WORM FLY *Cochliomyia hominivorax:* Any creature with a name like *hominivorax*—"eater of man"—is best avoided. U.S. agricultural officials knew this when, in 1958, they began an extraordinarily sophisticated campaign to eradicate the fly. They exposed male screw-worm flies to radiation, rendering them sterile, then released them throughout the South. Once those sterile males mated with females, the females would, in all probability, die without mating again, which would bring their life cycle to an end.

Thanks to those efforts, the screw-worm fly was entirely eliminated from the United States, with only sporadic outbreaks that have been fairly easy to treat. This is good news for the livestock the flies were attacking—and for humans as well.

A pregnant female will lay two to three hundred eggs around a wound or at the edges of mucus membranes—in the eyes, ears, nose, mouth, or genitals of humans and other animals, including cattle. Once the eggs hatch and the larvae start feeding, more females are drawn to the site, and they, too, lay eggs. The larvae burrow deeply into the wound, earning them the name "screw-worm" for the way they screw themselves into the flesh and enlarge the wound, introducing the risk of infection. The larvae live inside their host for about a week, then drop to the ground to mature.

Any creature with a name like *hominivorax*— "eater of man" — is best avoided.

A 1952 case from central California illustrates the problem these flies once posed in the United States. A man who was lounging in his backyard kept swatting at a fly buzzing around his head. The fly disappeared momentarily, but then the man felt a strange itch in his nose. When he blew his nose, the fly came out. Over the next few days, one side of his face became so swollen that he went to the doctor. The doctor irrigated his nasal passages and washed out twenty-five maggots. It took eleven more days of irrigation to remove all two hundred maggots that resulted from the fly making one brief visit to the inside of the man's nose.

While the screw-worm fly is mostly a dim memory in the United States, it is still found in Central and South America. Another species, the Old World screw-worm *Chrysomya bezziana*, is found in Africa, southeast Asia, India, and the Middle East. Doctors have noticed that an increase in adventure sports and *The Amazing Race*–style treks through jungles and deserts have caused a new generation of Americans and Europeans to become reacquainted with the screw-worm fly.

SCUTTLE FLY *Megaselia scalaris:* This fly, which is found world-wide, gets its name from its habit of "scuttling" around with short, jerky motions. It has also earned the name "coffin fly," as one of many flies that are attracted to dead bodies. Unfortunately, it is found among the living, too.

Scuttle flies are also known for their horrid attraction to the urinary tract. Cases of urogenital myiasis—infestations of eggs and larvae in the urinary or genital areas by scuttle flies—have been documented in areas of poor hygiene, particularly when some sort of wound or infection was already present.

In 2004, an Iranian man working in Kuwait was injured when concrete at a building site fell on him. At the hospital, he was treated for fractures and lacerations. After two weeks, scuttle fly maggots emerged from his wound while the bandage was being changed. By calculating the age of the larvae, hospital administrators were able to determine that the man had been infected at the hospital, and that the flies had to have crawled under his bandage to lay their eggs.

TUMBU FLY *Cordylobia anthropophaga:* In sub-Saharan Africa, people dread the arrival of the tumbu fly, whose females lay up to three hundred eggs at a time in the sandy soil, preferably soil contaminated with excrement if they can find it. They are also drawn to clean laundry that has been hung out to dry, depositing their eggs on it. To kill the eggs, the locals who can afford it dry their clothes in a hot dryer or iron them before they get dressed.

Once the eggs hatch, the larvae are able to burrow into healthy, unbroken skin, often without their victim noticing or feeling any pain at all. Over the next few days, a nasty boil develops. If left untreated, the sore will itch and hurt and leak a vile fluid made up of a mixture of blood and the bodily waste of the larvae.

The larvae will leave on their own after two weeks if they aren't forcibly removed first. Although the tumbu fly is found only in Africa, cases have turned up elsewhere, presumably because the eggs hitched a ride on a blanket or article of clothing coming from the continent.

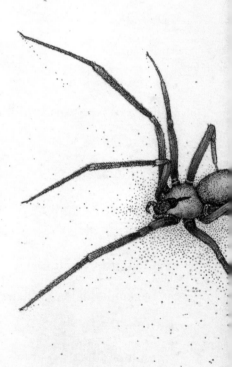

FEAR OF BUGS

Fear of anything is a *phobia*, which comes from the Greek word *phobus*. Psychologists officially recognize phobias only as a broad category and use the term to relate to any number of persistent and irrational fears. The practice of attaching a Greek or Latin word to *phobia* to create a more specific name for a particular fear was common in the nineteenth century but is no longer formally in use by psychologists. Here are just a few of the terms that have been invented to describe a fear of various bugs:

Acarophobia: Fear of mites or scabies

Arachnophobia: Fear of spiders

Apiphobia: Fear of bees

Cnidophobia: Fear of stings

Delusional parasitosis: Mistaken belief of infestation by parasites

Entomophobia: Fear of insects

Helminthophobia: Fear of being infested with worms

Isopterophobia: Fear of insects that eat wood

Katsaridaphobia: Fear of cockroaches

Lepidopterophobia: Fear of butterflies

Myrmecophobia: Fear of ants

Parasitophobia: Fear of parasites

Pediculophobia: Fear of lice

Scoleciphobia: Fear of parasitic worms

GLOSSARY

ANTIBIOTIC *(n)* a drug that is used to cure infections by killing bacteria

ANTIVENIN *(n)* a serum or liquid for the blood that is used to eliminate toxins or poisons; sometimes called antivenom

CREOSOTE *(n)* a chemical used to treat wood to protect it from rotting

ENTOMOLOGIST *(n)* a scientist who study insects

FAMILY *(n)* in biology, the grouping of related plants and animals that is larger than a genus but smaller than an order; creatures within the same family may look quite similar (for instance, dogs, wolves, and foxes are all members of the Canidae family)

GENUS *(n)* in biology, the grouping of related plants and animals that contains many species and is smaller than a family

HOST *(n)* the plant or animal that another organism lives in and feeds off of as a parasite

LARVA *(n)* a young, wormlike insect

MOLT *(v)* to lose the outer layer so that it can be replaced

NEMATODE *(n)* a cylindrical worm that lives off another organism or lives freely in the earth or water

NERVOUS SYSTEM *(n)* a system in the body made up of the brain, spinal cord, and nerves that controls everything the body does

NEUROTOXIN *(n)* a poison that affects the nervous system

NYMPH *(n)* the young form of an insect that looks like an adult but is not fully developed and does not have completely developed wings

ORDER *(n)* in biology, the grouping of plants and animals that is bigger than a family

PARASITE *(n)* a plant or animal that survives by living in or on another organism

PHEROMONE *(n)* a chemical substance that an animal or insect signals others with—often a scent

PROTOZOAN *(n)* a simple organism that is usually so small you can see it only with a microscope

PUPA *(n)* a young insect that has stopped eating and is protected with a cover, such as a cocoon; it is no longer a larva but not yet an adult

SPECIES *(n)* a group of plants and animals that is closely related, can create offspring, and has a two-part scientific name

VECTOR *(n)* an organism that transmits a disease or parasite from one animal or plant to another

RESOURCES

Visit www.WickedBugs.com for links to these and other online resources.

INSECT IDENTIFICATION

Making an accurate identification of an insect or insect bite is best left to the experts. Carefully capturing the insect or taking a good photograph of it is critical to identifying it. Armed with this information, contact your county agricultural extension office or the entomology department at your local university for assistance.

The Entomological Society of America (www.entsoc.org) offers a resource section on its website with links to entomological societies and other insect-related information.

The American Arachnological Society (www.american arachnology.org) offers a photo gallery, answers to commonly asked questions, and links to more resources.

BugGuide.net is an online community of insect enthusiasts who post pictures of insects, spiders, and other creatures.

INSECTARIUMS

Visiting an insectarium is a wonderful way to meet some of these creatures up close. Many natural history museums and zoos feature bug exhibits. Here are just a few of the more interesting insectariums around the world:

American Museum of Natural History, New York, NY (www.amnh.org) Holds one of the largest insect collections in the world. Insect-related exhibits are a regular feature.

Audubon Insectarium, New Orleans, LA (www.audubon institute.org) The first major institution to open in New Orleans after Hurricane Katrina; features live insect exhibits, a simulated underground encounter with human-sized bugs, and insect delicacies that brave children can sample in the cafeteria.

California Academy of Sciences, San Francisco, CA (www.calacademy.org) Features a four-story rain forest, natural history museum, educational naturalist center, and a living "green roof."

Field Museum, Chicago, IL (www.fieldmuseum.org) With an extraordinary insect and butterfly collection, also regularly features special insect exhibits.

Montreal Insectarium, Montreal, Quebec, Canada (http://espacepourlavie.ca/en/insectarium) Live and preserved specimens, butterfly exhibits, and special programs.

Natural History Museum of Los Angeles County, Los Angeles, CA (www.nhm.org) Has an insect zoo with live specimens, along with regular "bug shows" during which visitors can touch the creatures.

Natural History Museum, London, England (www.nhm.ac.uk) Known for its "creepy-crawly" exhibit, wildlife garden, and extraordinary Darwin Centre collection.

Smithsonian National Museum of Natural History, Washington, DC (www.mnh.si.edu) Includes an insect zoo, butterfly pavilion, and a vast collection of specimens.

PEST CONTROL

Correctly identifying pests is the first step to getting them out of your home and garden. Contact your county agricultural extension office or university entomology department for help identifying and controlling unwanted insects.

Almost every state has an integrated pest management (IPM) program to help eliminate pests using low-toxic approaches. Do a search online for your state's program. For instance, the Illinois program can be found at ipm.illinois.edu.

Pesticide Action Network North America (www.panna.org) offers a pesticide information database and information about alternatives to pesticides.

Richard Fagerlund (askthebugman.com) has been delivering sensible and safe pest control advice for years through his syndicated "Ask the Bugman" column and now through his website.

INSECT-TRANSMITTED DISEASES

The Centers for Disease Control (www.cdc.gov) offers advice for travelers to minimize exposure to insect-transmitted disease and provides basic overviews of many of those diseases.

The World Health Organization (www.who.int) monitors and fights insect-transmitted disease outbreaks worldwide and offers basic health information for travelers.

The Carter Center (www.cartercenter.org) is working to eliminate a number of the diseases described in this book. The organization's strategies include teaching people how to build healthier latrines, distributing water filters, and offering free medication. Even a small donation can save a life; visit the website to find out more.

BIBLIOGRAPHY

IDENTIFICATION GUIDES

Capinera, John L., ed. *Encyclopedia of Entomology*. Dordrecht, Netherlands: Springer, 2008.

Eaton, Eric R., and Kenn Kaufman. *Kaufman Field Guide to Insects of North America*. Kaufman field guide. New York: Houghton Mifflin Harcourt, 2007.

Evans, Arthur V. *National Wildlife Federation Field Guide to Insects and Spiders and Related Species of North America*. New York: Sterling, 2007.

Foster, Steven, and Roger A. Caras. *A Field Guide to Venomous Animals and Poisonous Plants: North America, North of Mexico*. Peterson field guide series, 46. Boston: Houghton Mifflin Harcourt, 1994.

Haggard, Peter, and Judy Haggard. *Insects of the Pacific Northwest*. Timber Press field guide. Portland, OR: Timber Press, 2006.

Levi, Herbert Walter, Lorna Rose Levi, Herbert S. Zim, and Nicholas Strekalovsky. *Spiders and Their Kin*. New York: Golden Press, 1990.

O'Toole, Christopher, ed. *Firefly Encyclopedia of Insects and Spiders*. Toronto: Firefly Books, 2002.

Resh, Vincent H., and Ring T. Cardé, eds. *Encyclopedia of Insects*. San Diego: Academic Press, 2009.

MEDICAL REFERENCES

Goddard, Jerome. *Physician's Guide to Arthropods of Medical Importance*. Boca Raton, FL: CRC Press, 2007.

Lane, Richard P., and Roger Ward Crosskey, eds. *Medical Insects and Arachnids*. London: Springer, 1993.

Mullen, Gary R., and Lance Durden, eds. *Medical and Veterinary Entomology*. Amsterdam: Academic Press, 2002.

PEST CONTROL

Ellis, Barbara W., and Fern Marshall Bradley, eds. *The Organic Gardener's Handbook of Natural Insect and Disease Control: A Complete Problem-Solving Guide to Keeping Your Garden and Yard Healthy without Chemicals*. Emmaus, PA: Rodale Press, 1996.

Gillman, Jeff. *The Truth About Garden Remedies: What Works, What Doesn't, and Why*. Portland, OR: Timber Press, 2008.

Gillman, Jeff. *The Truth About Organic Gardening: Benefits, Drawbacks, and the Bottom Line*. Portland, OR: Timber Press, 2008.

INDEX

Note: Page numbers in *italics* refer to illustrations.

A

acarophobia, 164
Acrididae, 79
African bat bug, *62,* 63–64
African bombardier beetle, 119
Afrocimex constrictus, 62, 63–64
alarm pheromone, 39
American cockroach, 29
Ampulex compressa, 71
Androctonus crassicauda, 26
Anobiidae, 75
Anopheles sp., 16, 17–19
antibiotic, 165
antivenin, 165
Antommarchi, Francesco Carlo, 113
ants, x, 127–32
aphids, x
apiphobia, 164
Apis cerana japonica, 98
arachnids, x
arachnologists, 105
arachnophobia, 164
archduke caterpillar, 124
Archispirostreptus gigas, 67
Argentine ant, 128–29
Arizona bark scorpion, 25
ascariasis, 52
Ascaris lumbricoides, 51–52
Asian giant hornet, *96,* 97–99
asp moth, 126
assassin bugs, *10,* 11–14, 39
Atkins, John, 7
Auchmeromyia senegalensis, 159
Automeris io, 125–26

B

Backshall, Steve, 129
Baghdad Boil, 149
bald-faced hornet, 132

banana spider, 5
Barbary Plague, 22–23
bark beetles, 83
bat bugs, 37, *62,* 63–64
bed bug, *36,* 37–39
bed bugs, 63
beetles, *74,* 75–77, *82,* 83–85, 92–93,
    100, 101–3, *116,* 117–19
bird bugs, 37
biting midge, 147
Black Death, 21–23
black fly, *150,* 151–53
blacklegged tick, 34
black widow, *134,* 135–37
Blattella germanica, 28, 29–31
Blattellidae, 29
blindness, 151, 153
blocking, 22, 23
blow flies, 92
blue stain fungus, 84
body lice, *40,* 41–43, 45
bombardier beetle, *116,* 117–19
Bonaparte, Napoleon, 113–15
Brachinus, 118–19
Brazilian wandering spider, *2,* 3–5
Brothers, Vincent, 91
brown marmorated stink bug,
    58, 59–61
brown recluse, *104,* 105–7
Brugia malayi, 49–50
bug (term), x
bugs, fear of, 164
Bulkley, L. D., 43
bullet ant, 129, 132
bullhorn acacia ant, 132
burying beetles, 92–93

C

Calliphora, 92
Calliphoridae, 92
Carabidae, 117
carrion flies, 92
Carter, Jimmy, 49, 157
Carter Center, 157
castor bean tick, 35
caterpillars, 123–26

cat flea, 21
centipedes, x, 39, 67, *108,* 109–11
Centruroides sculpturatus, 25
Chagas, Carlos, 13–14
Chagas disease, 12–14
Chicago Daily Tribune, ix
chigger mite, *142,* 143–45
chigoe flea, *138,* 139–41
Chrysomya bezziana, 161
cigarette beetle, 75
Cimex lectularius, 36, 37–39
Cimicidae, 37, 63
classification, scientific, xi
Cleridae, 93
cnidophobia, 164
cobweb spiders, 135
Cochliomyia hominivorax, 160–61
cockroach, *28,* 29–31, 71
coffin fly, 162
Columbus, Christopher, 139
Congo floor maggot, 159
Coptotermes formosanus, 86, 87–89
Cordylobia anthropophaga, 162–63
corpse eaters, 90–93
creosote, 165
Ctenidae, 3
Ctenocephalides canis, 21
Ctenocephalides felis, 21
Ctesias, 103
Culicidae, 17
Curculionidae, 83
cutaneous leishmaniasis, 148, 149
Cymothoa exigua, 72

D

Darwin, Charles, 11–12, 14, 117
deathstalker, 26
death-watch beetle, *74,* 75–77
decomposition, ix–x
deer tick, *32,* 33–35
delusional parasitosis, 164
Dendroctonus frontalis, 83
Dendroctonus ponderosae, 82, 83–85
dengue fever, 18
Dermatobia hominis, 159–60
Dermestidae, 93

detritivores, 67
devil's coach-horse beetle, 101
dog flea, 21
Dorylus sp., 130
dracunculiasis, 48
Dracunculus medinensis, 48–49
driver ant, 130
drugstore beetle, 75

E

earthworms, 55–57
Eisenia fetida, 55
elephantiasis, 49–50
emerald cockroach wasp, 71
entomologists, x, 165
entomophobia, 164
epilepsy, 51
erythema migrans, 35
European black millipede, *66,* 67–69
European hornet, 97, 132
European worms, 56–57

F

family, 165
fattail scorpion, 26
fear of bugs, 164
filth fly, *154,* 155–57
fire ant, 72, 130–32
fire caterpillar, 124–25
fish, 72
flannel moth, 126
fleas, *20,* 21–23, *138,* 139–41
flies, *6,* 7–9, 72, 92, *146,* 147–49, *150,*
    151–53, *154,* 155–57, 159–63
Fogle, Ben, 147, 148
food, insects as, ix
forensic entomology, 90–91
Formosan subterranean termite,
    86, 87–89

G

gamasid mites, 93
genus, xi, 165
giant African millipede, 67

giant centipede, *108,* 109–11
giant redheaded centipede, 111
Glomeris marginata, 69
Glossina morsitans, 8
Glossina palpalis, 8
Glossina sp., 6, 7–9
Glossina tachinoides, 8
Glossinidae, 7
grasshoppers, 72, 79–81
green-banded broodsac, 71
Grose, Francis, 76
guinea worm, 48–49
guinea worm disease, 48–49
gypsy moth caterpillar, 125

H

hairworm, 72
Hale, Cindy, 55–57
Halyomorpha halys, 58, 59–61
ham beetles, 93
Hargis, Carole, 121
Hargis, David, 121
harvest mites, 143
head lice, 41, *44,* 45–46
helminthophobia, 164
Hemiptera, x
Henderson, Gregg, 88
honeybee, 98–99, 132
hornet, 132
hornet juice, 99
hornets, *96,* 97–99
host, 51, 165
house centipede, 39
house fly, 155
human bot fly, 159–60
humans
    parasites affecting, 47–52
    scientific classification of, xi
Hunter, Mark, 87
Hurricane Katrina, 87–89

I

"If Bugs Were the Size of Men," ix
insectariums, 167–68
insect identification resources, 167

insects, ix–x
insect-transmitted diseases, 169
International Atomic Energy Agency, 9
io moth caterpillar, 125–26
Ips typographus, 83
isopterophobia, 164
Ixodes pacificus, 35
Ixodes ricinus, 35
Ixodes scapularis, 32, 33–35
Ixodidae, 33

J

jewel wasp, 71
Julidae, 67
Justinian's plague, 23
juvenile rheumatoid arthritis, 34

K

katsaridaphobia, 164
Kimsey, Lynn, 91
"kissing bug," 13
Küchenmeister, Friedrich, 47

L

LaFage, Jeffery, 88
larva, 165
Lasioderma serricorne, 75
latrodectism, 137
Latrodectus, 135
Latrodectus hasselti, 136
Latrodectus hesperus, 134, 135–37
leaf-footed bugs, 59
leishmaniasis, 148–49
Leiurus quinquestriatus, 26
Lenin, Vladimir, 42
lepidopterophobia, 164
Leptotrombidium sp., 142, 143–45
Leucochloridium paradoxum, 71
Lexias spp., 124
Liarsky, Stephen, 135–36
lice, *40,* 41–43, *44,* 45–46, 50, 72
Linepithema humile, 128–29
locust plagues, 79–81
locusts, *78,* 79–81

London Zoo, 135–36
Lonomia achelous, 124–25
Lonomia obliqua, 124–25
Loxosceles reclusa, 104, 105–7
Lumbricidae, 55
Lumbricus rubellus, 55, 56
Lumbricus terrestris, 54, 55–57
Lymantria dispar, 125
Lyme disease, 33–35
lymphatic filariasis, 49–50

M
maggots, 158–63
malaria, 17–19
masked hunter, 39
Mastigoproctus giganteus, 26
mating lek, 148
medicine, insects used in, x
Megalopyge opercularis, 126
Megaselia scalaris, 162
Melanoplus spretus, 78, 79–81
Merck, 153
millipedes, *66,* 67–69
mites, 50, 93, *112,* 113–15, *142,*
    143–45
mold mites, 93
molt, 165
mosquitoes, xi, *16,* 17–19
moths, 126
mountain pine beetle, *82,* 83–85
mucocutaneous leishmaniasis, 148
Murray, Polly, 33–34
Musca domestica, 155
Musca sorbens, 154, 155–57
Muscidae, 155
myrmecophobia, 164

N
Nairobi eye, 102
Nairobi flies, 101
names, scientific, xi
Napoleon Bonaparte, 41
nematode, 165
nervous system, 166
neurotoxin, 166

Nicrophorus, 92
nightcrawler, *54,* 55–57
nymph, 166

O
Ocypus olens, 101
Old World screw-worm, 161
Ommatoiulus moreletii, 68
Onchocerca volvulus, 152
Ono, Masato, 97, 98
order, 166
oriental rat flea, *20,* 21–23
Orientia tsutsugamushi, 144
Orthoporus dorsovittatus, 68, 69
Oviedo, Francisco de, 139

P
Paederus beetle, *100,* 101–3
Paederus dermatitis, 101–2
Paederus sp., 100, 101–3
palmetto bug, 29
paper wasp, 132
Paraponera clavata, 129, 132
parasites, 47–52, 166
parasitophobia, 164
pederin, 101, 103
Pediculidae, 41, 45
pediculophobia, 164
pediculosis corporis, 42
Pediculus humanus capitis, 44, 45–46
Pediculus humanus corporis, 40, 41–43
Pediculus humanus humanus, 40, 41–43
Pentatomidae, 59
Periplaneta americana, 29
pest control resources, 169
pesticides, x, 31, 38, 153
pheromones, 83, 97, 98, 166
Phlebotomus sp., 146, 147–49
phobias, 164
Phoenix Children's Hospital, 25
Phoneutria sp., 2, 3–5
phorid fly, 72
pill millipede, 67
plague, 21–23
Poe, Edgar Allan, 75

pollination, ix
pork tapeworm, 50–51
protozoan, 8, 13, 148, 166
A Provincial Glossary (Grose), 76
Psalmopoeus cambridgei, 122
Pseudacteon spp., 72
Psychodidae, 147
Pulicidae, 21
pupa, 166
puss caterpillar, 126

R

Randall's Island, 155–56
recluse spiders, 105
redback spider, 136
red harvester ant, 132
red imported fire ant, 130
Reduviidae, 11
Reduvius personatus, 39
red wiggler, 55
red worm, 55, 56
Rhinotermitidae, 87
Rift Valley fever, 18
Rocky Mountain locust, *78,* 79–81
Rocky Mountain spotted fever, 35
roundworms, 50–52
rove beetles, 93, 101

S

sand fly, *146,* 147–49
Sarcoptes scabiei canis, 113
Sarcoptes scabiei var. hominis, 112,
　113–15
sarcoptic mange, 113
Sarcoptidae, 113
Sateré-Mawé tribe, 129
scabies, 113–15
scabies mite, 50, *112,* 113–15
Schmidt, Justin, 132
Schmidt Sting Pain Index, 132
scientific classification, x, xi
scoleciphobia, 164
Scolopendra gigantean, 108, 109–11
Scolopendra heros, 111
Scolopendridae, 109

scorpions, x, *24,* 24–26
screw-worm fly, 160–61
scrub typhus, 143–45
Scutigera coleoptrata, 39
scuttle fly, 162
Sicariidae, 105
Simuliidae, 151
simuliotoxicosis, 152
Simulium damnosum, 150, 151–53
six-eyed sand spider, 105
skin beetles, 93
sleeping sickness, 7–9
Sleepy Distemper, 7
slugs, x
snails, 71
Solenopsis invicta, 130–32
southern pine beetle, 83
southern tick-associated rash illness, 35
sp., xi
species, 166
species names, xi
spiders, x, *2,* 3–5, *104,* 105–7, *134,*
　135–37
Spinochordodes tellinii, 72
spp., xi
spruce bark beetle, 83
stable flies, 155
Stanley, Henry Morton, 8
Staphylinidae, 93, 101
Steere, Allen, 34
Stegobium paniceum, 75
Stenaptinus insignis, 116, 117–19
sterile insect technique, 9
stinging caterpillars, 123–26
Sting Pain Index, 132
stink bugs, *58,* 59–61
suicide, by black widow, 135–36
sweat bee, 132

T

Tachypodoiulus niger, 66, 67–69
Taenia solium, 50–51
Takahaski, Naoko, 99
tangle-web spiders, 135
tapeworms, 21, 47, 50–51
tarantism, 122

tarantula, *120*, 121–22
tarantula hawk, 132
"The Tell-Tale Heart" (Poe), 75
termites, 87
Theraphosa blondi, 120, 121–22
Theraphosidae, 121
Theridiidae, 135
thread-legged bugs, 11
tick fever, 35
ticks, *32,* 33–35
Tityus trinitatis, 26
tongue-eating louse, 72
trachoma, 156
trench fever, 41
Triatoma infestans, 10, 11–14
Trinidad scorpion, 26
Trombiculidae, 143
true bugs, x
trypanosomiasis, 8
tsetse fly, *6,* 7–9
tsutsugamushi fever, 144
tularemia, 35
tumbu fly, 162–63
Tunga penetrans, 138, 139–41
tungiasis, 140–41
Tungidae, 139
typhus, 41–43
tyroglyphid mites, 93

U
Uvarov, Boris, 80–81

V
vagabond disease, 42
vector, 166
ventilated improved pit latrine (VIP),
   157
Vespa crabro, 97
Vespa mandarinia japonica, 96, 97–99
Vespidae, 97
vinegarroon, 26
visceral leishmaniasis, 148, 149

W
wandering spiders, 4
The Washing Away of Wrongs, 90
Washington, George, 17
wasps, 71, 97, 132
weevils, 83
West Indian tarantula, 122
wheel bugs, 11
whip scorpion, 26
worms, x, 47–52, 55–57, 71, 72, 161
Wuchereria bancrofti, 49–50

X
Xenopsylla cheopis, 20, 21–23
Xestobium rufovillosum, 74, 75–77

Y
yak-killer hornet, 97
yellow fever, 18
yellowjacket, 132

Z
Zinsser, Hans, 43
zombie bugs, 70–72

AMY STEWART is the author of eight books, including the *New York Times* bestsellers *Wicked Plants* and *Wicked Bugs*. She and her husband live in Eureka, California, where they own a bookstore called Eureka Books. Visit her online at amystewart.com and find her on Twitter: @Amy_Stewart.